JACKIE HILL PERRY

GAY GIRL, GOOD GOD

The Story of Who I Was and Who God Has Always Been

B&H
PUBLISHING
BRENTWOOD, TENNESSEE

978-1-4627-5122-8

Published by B&H Publishing Group
Brentwood, Tennessee

Dewey Decimal Classification: 248.843
Subject Heading: CHRISTIAN LIFE

9 10 11 12 13 14 • 27 26 25 24 23

Dedicated to . . .

God
Preston
Eden
Mother
Santoria
Brian
Melody

Contents

JACKIE HILL PERRY

Acknowledgments

THANK YOU, PRESTON, FOR supporting me. Thank you, Nancy, for encouraging me. Thank you, Robert, Austin, Devin, and B&H, for guiding me. Thank you, friends (you know who you are), for praying for me.

Foreword

JACKIE HILL PERRY AND I could hardly have more disparate backgrounds.

She is a millennial; I am a Boomer. She is black, and I am white. She was raised by a single mom and disregarded by an absentee dad who had no idea how to love her. I was parented by a happily married, attentive mom and dad who adored each other and their children. Jackie is sixteen years younger than her brother and only sibling, while I have six younger brothers and sisters.

Jackie is a hip-hop artist. I have a degree in piano performance, zero sense of rhythm, and gravitate toward music written before 1910. She is a poet who uses words—with amazing deftness—to paint pictures on the canvas of the heart that are at once provocative and evocative. My speaking and writing style tends toward sequential points, neatly organized and outlined.

Jackie had her first homosexual experience when she was in high school. I don't recall ever hearing the word *homosexual* or knowing anyone who identified as one, until sometime after I was out of high school. She didn't meet Jesus till she was in her late teens; my first conscious memory is trusting Christ to save me at the age of four.

My association with Jackie has introduced me to, among other things, an expanded vocabulary. I remember, for example, the day she and I were direct messaging about a ministry she was serving with at the time. She informed me it was "a pretty dope ministry." To which I replied: "Dope??" Somehow, I was unaware (as she graciously explained) that "dope is a slang word for awesome or great." ("Had me confused," I responded. "Glad they're not doing dope!") We both had a good laugh.

Yes, ours has been an unlikely friendship. Yet, different as we are in many respects, our lives and hearts have been knit together through our common need for a Savior and the lavish grace we have both received from Christ. Beyond that, we share a love for God's Word, and we both cherish and cling to sound doctrine as being not only true and necessary, but also beautiful and good. All of this, combined with observing her depth of discernment and wisdom and the ways God is using her bold, clear voice, has made me a cheerleader for Jackie (and her husband Preston).

In God's providence, two of my books, *Lies Women Believe and the Truth that Sets Them Free* and *Seeking Him* (coauthored with Tim Grissom), played a significant role in Jackie's discipleship as a young believer. In more recent years, her writing, speaking, and social media activity have been a part of my own discipleship and have deepened my love for Christ and my appreciation for the difference the gospel makes in every part and particle of our lives. So I was honored when Jackie asked if I would write a foreword for her first book.

As I read her manuscript, I found myself repeatedly interrupting my sweet husband, who was seated at my side, working on his laptop, to share with him sentences and paragraphs that had me spellbound. "She sees things others don't," Robert said. He's right. And she describes those things in ways most of us can't.

I'll admit I flinched a bit when I first heard the proposed title for this book. *"Gay girl"* I pushed back mentally—*but that's not who she is today!* Which, as I was drawn into the manuscript, I came to understand is precisely the point. Jackie is honest and raw in her depiction of "who she was," which provides the perfect backdrop to spotlight and celebrate "who God has always been." Her understanding and expression of both—her fallenness and brokenness and His redeeming love and grace—are solidly grounded in truth, as He has revealed it in His Word.

This is not a book to be skimmed or speed read, but one to be savored and pondered, as Jackie looks through the lens of Scripture and her own journey to unpack such realities as fatherlessness, abuse, same-sex attraction, identity, temptation, fighting lust with the gospel, and misconceptions of womanhood. Throughout, she points to a Savior who loves sinners and a gospel that saves, transforms, and keeps those who come to Him in repentance and faith—however similar or dissimilar their story may be from hers.

As Jackie concludes:

> "What God has done to my soul is worth telling because He is worth knowing. Worth seeing. Worth hearing. Worth loving, and trusting, and exalting. . . . To tell you about what God has done for my soul is to invite you into my worship."

So come and see, hear, love, trust, and exalt. Come and worship.

Nancy DeMoss Wolgemuth

September 2018

Introduction

I WROTE THIS BOOK out of love—a common word used so out of context on most days. This work is not a miscommunication of my intentions; it is a direct product of it.

Before writing it, I lived out the words. A gay girl once? Yes. Now? I am what God's goodness will do to a soul once grace gets to it.

In saying that, I know I've already offended someone. I don't assume that every hand that holds this book will agree with every black letter on the pages. There are many who, while reading, won't understand gayness as something possible of being in the past tense. It is either who you are, or what you have never been. To this, I disagree. The only constant in this world is God. Gayness, on the other hand, can be an immovable identity only when the heart is unwilling to bow. There is more complexity to this than my modest introduction will allow. I will only encourage those hesitant to turn the page because of my particular perspective on truth to keep reading. I'll admit that I have much more to say about gayness and

God that will be a bit countercultural, but I hope will also be intriguing to the point of consideration in the grand scheme of things.

There are others who only know of the hetero love that makes a book such as this one for studying the unknown. These are the Christians (the "I've always been straight" Christians, that is) for whom this book was also intended. I have not always loved how they've loved the gay community. Between the banner-painted hate and the interpersonal silence, my love for the church moved me to attempt to write something of balance—something that can make the love for which they are called to walk in, the tangible proof of what God is like.

This book, however, is not to be confused with the Scriptures themselves. It, God willing, will be of benefit to the church, but these words are not to be esteemed as being what is most important for the church. That is what the Word of God is for. This is not an appendix to the Scriptures; it is simply the telling of a story impacted by the Scriptures, with practical instruction gained by living out the Scriptures. My love for the LGBT community makes me desperate for them to know God. My love for the church makes me desperate for them to show the world God, as He is, and not as we would prefer for Him to be—this book being my efforts toward such an end. Coming out of the gay lifestyle and into a brand-new world of loving God *His* way is a wild life—a wildness so sufficient that it will either turn a new saint back or make them into someone better. If I were to call the experience by another adjective, I would call it "hard." A hardness much like a mountain too beat-up by the sky to climb. But even they can be moved.

For those saints, my love is a gathering up of my life, failures, victories, and everything I've figured out about God, edited and made into text for them to read. As they do, a deep "She gets it" might well up. But even better would be a "God is good," only to be followed by an "All the time!" from within. They are the demonstration of how often God saves. That there are more gay girls and boys that have been made new by a good God. For them, these words landed face-first that they may know that they are not alone.

In writing this book, I did it as myself. Meaning, I am as honest as I know how to be. I have never been one for pretense. When, as a new Christian, I was introduced to the typical nature in which some Christians speak of their lives in the loveliest terms, I refused to give in to the convenient misery of being ambiguous about the truth. If the truth is what sets us free, then why not walk in it at all times? With wisdom and love, of course, but also with the reality that truth is where freedom begins.

Finally, in this book you're holding, every sentence is the pursuit of showing off God. Leaving this word-filled place with a developed understanding of me and a shallow revelation of

God would make all of my efforts worthless. This is a book with a lot of me in it but with a whole lot more of God. He is what the soul needs for rest and what the mind needs for peace. He is the Creator God, the King of Glory, the one who, in love, sent the Christ to pay the penalty for and become the sin that we are all born with. It is the words from and about this resurrected Lamb of God that I hope will lift off the page and into the heart. This book is a lifted hand, a glad praise, a necessary hymn, a hallelujah overheard and not kept quiet. This work is my worship unto God that, with prayer, I hope will leave you saying, "God is *so* good!"

Jackie Hill Perry

PART 1

Who I Was

CHAPTER 1

2006

JACKIE, YOU WANNA BE my girlfriend?" she asked me, squinting like she knew her question might be offensive.

I'd seen her before. Back in middle school, she was one of the few who didn't hide their lesbianism in hallways, class-rooms, or wherever else conversations were held. If you knew anything about her family, you knew those hips belonged to her mama. She wore her identity with a smile, a smile that sat on top of her skin, skin that looked like bronze that had sat in the sun too long. I noticed it and the body she constantly called attention to.

It was the high school dance, and we were both standing in the middle of the gym floor turned dance hall. On one side, near the entrance, you could see a group of girls too popular for kindness. They laughed like everything was an inside joke and watched all who walked past for the sole purpose of making fun of what they saw. Across from them, underneath the glare of swirling party lights were last year's homecoming king, and all the other boys whom girls flocked to dance in front of. They were hoping that one of the boys would detach himself from his clique and ask one of them for their phone number. If she was pretty enough, he might even remember her name when he called. But for now, the boys loved the feeling of having their ego lifted on a Saturday night.

We stood in the middle of the room. I could tell she was growing impatient. I hadn't answered her question yet or even let my body tell her what my mouth wanted to say. All I could think about was Monday, and what it would have in store for me if I said "yes" to her invitation. The news wouldn't walk but run toward every ear and fly out of every mouth that heard it—until the school no longer saw me as the girl that had a smart mouth and a timid frame but as, "The gay girl."

They'd say my name like it was contagious. Like what I was would rub off on their skin, crawl inside of their little heterosexual hearts, and meddle with it until they ended up just as "sick" as I was.

I thought about the violent ones the most. They came from the same breed as the popular girls in the corner. It was a gift of theirs to use words as weapons and never discard them even if it killed everyone they spoke to. Gay slurs were their favorites. They concealed and carried them everywhere they went. Unloading one wouldn't be a challenge. I saw her face and I

GAY GIRL, GOOD GOD

heard the sound of a pistol being loaded. She was still waiting, intrigued by my silence. I thought I could hear bullets ricochet off the floor and tell me to be quiet.

"Girl, don't play with me like that! I ain't gay." I sounded so straight. On purpose. I'd come to the homecoming dance to take part in the traditional teenage revelry that these nights were made for. My clothes, purchased with twenty hours of weekend work, were put on to draw attention to me, but she was after more than I was willing to pay. She wanted me, and probably expected me, to take her up on her offer. But to me, that would've been no different than unclothing in front of a crowd. I was not willing to undress my secrets in front of her or anybody else for that matter. For now, I was okay with the fantasy of being honest. At least I knew it would keep me warm.

CHAPTER 2

6,000 BC–AD 1995

I WAS ATTRACTED TO women before I knew how to spell my name. My mama had given it to me. She thought it sounded dignified. Like a spine unwilling to bend. She'd heard it often in her younger days every time John F. Kennedy's wife was mentioned in the news. As for me, in second grade, I didn't know who the 35th president had been or what wife he'd let stand beside him as he waved to the world. All I knew was that our name had too many letters in it, and that my teeth had a small gap in them, reasons for which my ancestors were to blame, and that—according to my teacher—I asked too many questions.

When I looked at the sky, I didn't understand why it wasn't the color of my hands, instead of looking like my teacher's eyes. And why that one girl, who sat two desks over, made me feel weird. Or why my heart moved whenever she did. Or how, during recess, we'd end up in the corner of a Fisher-Price cabin, doing things we'd never seen, making sure our doing so remained as such.

The roof reminded me of a crayon—the green kind that you brought out of the box only when you needed to draw grass. The cabin itself was a boring version of brown, with the only excitement being the bright mustard yellow shutters that framed the plastic window cutouts we kept closed while inside. Without being taught to, we hid ourselves. Somehow, our minds carried rules that our hearts knew we were breaking. My mama was at work and when she thought about me, she probably envisioned my not-yet-guarded eyes, full of glee as I ran across the jungle gym like a brand-new lion dressed in a red shirt and blue jean shorts. With hair, dark and thick as my father's pride, swinging in the wind, until it was time to go back to class and learn how to write. She didn't know I was learning *other* things. And how what I was feeling hadn't told me its name yet. All I knew was, I had to keep *it* to myself.

———

Parents can't help but pass down things to their children. Every time I stood next to my mama, some joke we could both catch on to got ahold of our mouths—it would crack open and let a laugh out. Behind it, you'd see that gap and know we were related. That she'd given me, what had been hers all of her life, only because I was born wearing her genes.

Way before my mama had a mouth to smile with, or her mama had hands to clean collard greens (hands that came from a woman who had a slave's eyes, a stolen African's cheekbones, and a European's last name)—there were the two people to see God's face first. Adam and Eve looked much different back then. I'm sure they stood as tall and as strong as God had intended, with almost glorious skin, just like the baby they never had to be. But how they looked had more to do with whom they reflected than how attractive they might've been. When made, their bodies and their souls were unblemished— clean, almost glass-like through which to see their Creator. He couldn't be compared to anything other than Himself, nor easily described by the things He'd made. Words like *gorgeous, amazing, wonderful,* or *breathtaking* are easy, borderline lazy when used to describe the Holy One.

If, over coffee, we could ask Adam what word came to his mind the moment after he exhaled and saw God for the first time, he'd probably say, "Good. I saw Him and knew He was *good.*" Somebody who'd been born after Adam would most likely say under their breath, as not to seem irreverent, "Good? That's the best word he could come up with to describe God? Heck, even *I'm* good." The doubt whispered was the familiar smile, the identical eyes, the matching cheekbones, and the busy hands. And it was Adam, and not God, that had passed that down to us all.

It all started after Adam's wife, Eve, who had been made from a rib in his side, started having conversations with one of the animals her husband had named. The serpent, as Adam determined it should be called, was slick. He had the kind of character that an elderly woman, who'd been burned twice and never again, would sniff out as soon as it walked in the room. It's not mentioned if, when the serpent approached Eve, he had the decency to introduce himself. Telling her his name might've confused her or worse, given her the chance to ask him where he'd come from. Adam named it *serpent*, but the one speaking was known by every demon in hell as Satan. Being smarter than that, he stuck to asking only questions first. They could save the "getting to know you" portion for later.

Not being one for small talk, he went straight to questioning her about something God told her husband a little after He made him. God, after making the heavens, the earth, and everything in it, put Adam in Eden's garden. What surrounded Adam were trees, and lots of them—all pleasant to look at and good to eat from. In the middle, there was one that wasn't any more spectacular than the rest, but just as beautiful as them all, named "The tree of the knowledge of good and evil." Adam was told that all of the trees were his to enjoy. Seeing that God Himself planted them for his delight, they would produce the best fruit he'd ever taste. Every bite would remind him of the goodness he'd seen the day he came alive. However, to bite from the tree of the knowledge of good and evil would kill him. God told him that would be the case and as holiness would have it, He wasn't lying when He said it.

As a child, I might've needed to learn how to write. Or how to put nine letters together and spin them into my first name, but nobody had to teach me about joy. I came out of the womb already built to take it in. The first sip of milk clashed against my newborn taste buds before it fell into my brand-new belly. As it did, I was not only satisfied by being full but by experiencing the taste of food. A small smile grew from within because of it. Growing older, I found other joys such as friends, cartoons, sleepovers, carnivals, hugs, toys, Snickers, Christmas morning, and laughter. God's goodness spread out through all that He'd made, including me, giving me the capacity to enjoy image-bearers and what their hands created. Joy has never been the problem. It was our hearts that bent us away from finding our ultimate enjoyment in Who'd made us, which crippled how, what, and who we got joy from.

Back in the garden with Eve, the serpent starting speaking:

> "Did God actually say, 'You shall not eat of any tree in the garden'?" And the woman said to the serpent, "We may eat of the fruit of the trees in the garden, but God said, 'You shall not eat of the fruit of the tree that is in the midst of the garden,

neither shall you touch it, lest you die.'" But the serpent said to the woman, "You will not surely die. For God knows that when you eat of it your eyes will be opened, and you will be like God, knowing good and evil." So when the woman saw that the tree was good for food, and that it was a delight to the eyes, and that the tree was to be desired to make one wise, she took of its fruit and ate, and she also gave some to her husband who was with her, and he ate. Then the eyes of both were opened, and they knew that they were naked. And they sewed fig leaves together and made themselves loincloths. (Genesis 3:1–7)

What the devil had in mind when he picked Eve's brain was not necessarily a matter of wondering what answer she'd give. It wasn't even the question itself that she should've been wary of, it was the *way* in which it began. "Did God *actually* say . . ." Or to be said another way "Was God telling the truth?" The question was a subtle indictment on the character of God in which, if believed, would draw Eve away from seeing Him rightly. A lying God couldn't be trusted, let alone worshiped. He'd only say things He didn't really mean or make claims He'd never be able to fulfill.

Satan then tells her, after she fails to rebuke, that God is more like the devil than she might've known. By promising her immortality even after disobedience (though God had warned death), Satan was framing God as a liar, and himself as the bearer of truth—that God's Word was as fickle as a promise in the mouth of a con artist. He promised that she'd be able to sin and still remain alive. That God's holiness, and goodness, and glory, were all a sham. Only to be fully discovered by doing what He commanded she shouldn't.

Eve looked. The tree still stood. Before, it might've only been a part of the garden that caught her eye on rare occasions. Only to be overshadowed by all the glory God turned loose around it. It had always been forbidden to eat from, but never to touch. But, there were always better things to do, and eat, and touch, and sit on, and delight in, and live with. One tree being off limits was the least of their worries when they could see God every day. Until doubt came.

I imagine the tree looked different then. The fruit hung beneath their own branch, loose enough for the wind to move through each one. She noticed them and thought of her next meal. How they'd taste good on her plate, even if it meant she might not live to see the next chew. One blink later, her eyes saw how gorgeous the tree was. How it looked like God, only better, she thought. She remembered what the serpent had said about God, and how the tree would make her like Him. She figured fruit and not faith, sin and not obedience, would give her the wisdom she needed to be more perfect than she already was. Interestingly enough, some of what she saw was true. The tree was indeed good for food and pleasant to the sight; God had made it that way (Genesis 2:9). The deception was in believing that the tree was more satisfying to the body and more pleasurable to the sight than God. All of the wisdom she thought the tree could provide left her body the moment she did something foolish: Believe the devil.

To me, the devil made more sense than God sometimes. Both he and God spoke. God, through His Scriptures; Satan, through doubt. I'd learned of the Ten Commandments in Sunday school in between eating a handful of homemade popcorn and picking at my stockings. The "Thou shall nots" didn't complement the sweet buttered chew I found myself distracted by. They were a noise I didn't care to welcome. "You can't. You shouldn't. Do not," didn't sound like a song worth listening to, only a terrible noise to drown out by resistance. Satan, on the other hand, only told me to do what felt good, or what made sense to *me*. If lying allowed me to keep the belt in my mama's hand from tearing my behind in two, then lying was a *good* thing. I defined goodness on my own terms. It wore whatever definition I decided it should have on for the day. God had indeed been the original one to introduce the concept of goodness into the earth but for me to live in His kind of goodness, faith was required. All that He said was good *was* good because He was. Including all that He'd commanded me not to do, for He knew that the cruelest thing He could ever do was to not tell me and everyone alive to avoid what would keep us from Him.

Yet, unbelief doesn't see God as the ultimate good. So it can't see sin as the ultimate evil. It instead sees sin as a good thing and thus God's commands as a stumbling block to joy. In believing the devil, I didn't need a pentagram pendant to wear, neither did I need to memorize a hex or two. All I had to do was trust myself more than God's Word. I had to believe that my thoughts, my affections, my rights, my wishes, were worthy of absolute obedience and that in laying prostrate before the flimsy throne I'd made for myself, that I'd be doing a good thing.

After Adam (who'd been standing there with the wife he failed to protect from the serpent) ate from the tree, they died. Their bodies still stood, warm blood still pumped through their veins, eyes still let the light in. But what God said would come from disobedience, happened. Their refusal to trust Him over and above their inordinate affections, their distorted logic, and their desire for autonomy rendered them no longer friends of God but enemies. His holiness was actual. His judgment was real. And their knowledge of sin was now not just intellectual, but experiential.

Sin, when in the body, cannot not stay put. It's not a guest that stays in one room, making sure not to disturb the others. It is a tenant that lives in everything and goes everywhere. It can bleed into every part, choking out anything holy. The glass shattered and broke when it moved in. Adam and Eve, God's first image-bearers, made to love and reflect God in creation, had now become the world's first sinners.

Everyone born after Adam inherited it. And, just like Eve, I from birth, would experience the remnants of her dealings with the serpent. Being born human meant that I had the capacity for affection and logic. Being born sinful meant both were inherently broken. The unnamed attraction I felt at an elemental level only highlighted how greedy sin can be. Desires exist because God gave them to us. But homosexual desires exist because sin does. Loving Him, as we were created to do, involves both the will and the affections, but sin steals this love God placed in us for Himself and tells it to go elsewhere. Sin had taken ahold of the heart and turned it toward something lesser. Same-sex desires are actual. Though born of sin, they aren't an imaginary feeling one conjures up for the sake of being different. But the actuality of the affection doesn't make them morally justifiable. It is the mind, when conformed to the image of sin, that moves us to call evil good simply because it feels good to us.

Just as Eve let her body tell her what she should do with it, instead of God's Word, which would've reminded her of what it was made for, I was inevitably prone to the same kind of unbelief. The one in which sin seemed better than submission. Or where women, who are beautifully and wonderfully made, just as the tree had been, would be *more* beautiful and *more* wonderful than I considered God to be.

———

In that Fisher-Price cabin, it was a sure thing that I was my mama's baby. But the fruit hadn't fallen too far from the tree. What I did behind those bright yellow shutters and what I felt while trying to spell my name was only proof that I was also Adam's child.

CHAPTER 3

1988

EAST SAINT LOUIS WAS a hop, skip, and Mississippi River away from Saint Louis. Both cities sat inside of two different states but they always ended up sharing residents. Friday night is when it happened the most. Black twenty-to-thirty-somethings would make their way over the bridge that connected Missouri to Illinois, find a club worthy of their night, and dance. With the music louder than their mourning, they could forget the 9-to-5 they left at home and be as young as they wanted to be.

A woman, height barely breaking 5-foot-3, with the smile of a million laughs, and the eyes of one whose memories are cold and brutal to touch walked inside the club. She exhaled a sigh of relief when she stepped in and felt a little air move across her face. The July night had sent a little sweat down her temple. It worked to her advantage by making her look as if she'd stolen some of the moon's light and dressed her face with it. Her hair was off balance, on purpose. Cut in an asymmetrical style that mirrored every black woman alive in 1988. Moving the longer portion of her hair to the side, she scanned the room for an empty seat. Finding one, she sat in it, waiting for a friend while she enjoyed herself. It was as if she had no problem being her own company.

By the door, she recognized the guy walking in. The lights were dim but shined just enough to illuminate his face. It was hard not to take notice of his deep brown eyes and how they were fixed underneath a pair of long, dark eyebrows. One of which carried a scar down the middle. Maybe a sign that he had a habit of leaving things broken. He saw her, sitting with friends and he flashed a crooked smile her way. That smile made most women forget their common sense. But this woman was his boss, and ten years his senior. She was too grown to be desperate, but sensible enough to know he was fine.

A few weeks prior, they'd been introduced to each other by a mutual friend. He'd just gotten out of the Army and needed a civilian job. She managed a restaurant and was willing to give him a uniform he wouldn't have to learn how to shoot to put on. Initially, she was unimpressed by his presence. To her, he was no different than any other guy she had on her payroll until the night she saw him dressed like himself. Clocked out and smelling like an off-day, he had her attention.

From there, they became friends. They didn't go on dates; they went out to eat. Times when he'd stay over at her house and laugh the night away, they weren't spending time together, they were hanging out. And when they did, it was his mind that entertained her the most. When he spoke, she saw how much he was able to hold inside of it. She saw that it buried things—ideas, fears, facts, faces, fantasies that fell out only when he felt like talking. He asked questions she never knew she could answer. She learned more about her mind by interacting with his.

It wasn't safe to assume that his being around meant he was set on staying. Their friendship was made up of yarn strings destined to never come together. Yet, that didn't keep them from becoming one on occasion. Two months into being lovers, and never labeling their situation as that, she noticed that nothing she'd taken for her reoccurring nausea seemed to work. Two spoonfuls of Pepto-Bismol on a full stomach was clearly useless and not to mention, her jeans were continuing to either shrink, or her thighs were growing by the day. Assuming that menopause was the cause of her body's betrayal, she went to the doctor, only to discover that it wasn't menopausal hormones being abusive. I was growing inside of her.

"I want an abortion," my mother said. On the other end of the phone was her best friend. They'd known each other since they were four.

When Dwight D. Eisenhower was president and when many women had babies they didn't want or couldn't afford to keep but with no money to stop them from coming, they let 'em grow anyhow. The thick white extension cord sticking out from the bottom of the phone kept getting caught between her wrist and her forearm. She moved the phone to the other ear to let it unravel. It was adding to the frustration she felt burning in her hands. "I don't want the baby in *this* way."

What she meant was, she didn't want a baby *with him*. The coworker turned friend that became a lover. He was the "way" she never intended to bring another baby into the world by. Her first child, my brother, was already sixteen. She had him with a man she loved, and who loved her back. Her and my brother's father actually went on dates, made plans to spend time together, and called each other names like "Baby" and "Sweetie." My father was a twenty-five-year-old man, with a beautiful face but who had no idea how to sit still and love anything that would make him consistent. Their relationship was too complicated to bring a child into, she thought, so why not remove *it* or should I say, *me*.

Her best friend listened. She could hear the irrationality in my mother's argument. It being that abortion was to be considered instead of life. That removing me from the earth would make her own world better. Society had changed a whole lot since then but God was still the same. Abortion was still evil and had always been, even before the day "Thou shalt not kill" thundered out of God's mouth. She wasn't thinking clearly and her best friend had to help her see it for herself. She opened her mouth, and God spoke, "How do you know that God didn't intend for you to have the baby in *this way?*"

Like a cold glass of water to the face, my mother's eye widened, her heart beat truth into her chest, and the noise of death quieted down for a second. She had never considered providence and how involved it was with her womb. God, all-knowing, maker of man, creator of life, had orchestrated my conception. Though accomplished in sinful lusts, He had *given* me to her. He was forming me in her womb. Unbeknownst to her, He had chosen me before the foundation of the world to know Him. And no one—not my mother, my father, or even me—would get in His way.

CHAPTER 4

1989–2007

MY FATHER LOVED ME sometimes.

I didn't have the awareness to notice how far removed he was from me. Most children begin to remember nouns after pre-K. All persons, places, and things get their names etched into memory. Then, from there, nouns shape what they touch. Daddy, home, love became a contradiction once I realized how different my world looked from the picture books read to me during school. Dick and Jane had a father at home. Jackie didn't. Dick and Jane had a father to tuck them in. Jackie didn't. Dick and Jane woke up and ate breakfast with their Father. Jackie didn't. Jackie's father came to visit. Sometimes he didn't. Jackie's father called. Sometimes he didn't. Becoming sure of his absence came with better clarity during June, when my birthday and Father's Day were on the same date and neither me or my father said congratulations to one another. After a while, I stopped expecting him to. I figured he'd forgotten my birthdate anyway. That it was to him, the same as his cowork-ers grandchild's first day of school, too irrelevantly impersonal to move him to pleasure.

Wanting to save me from another disappointed sadness, my mother stopped getting me dressed for his arrival. Or telling me that the reason for my putting on ironed pants and a newly spin-dried shirt was that Daddy was about to pick me up. She was unwilling to participate in my heartbreak, so she stopped telling me about his promises altogether. There were far too many tears she'd removed from her daughter's face after my father never showed his. She'd grown tired of watching me stare at a closed door. Legs swinging to a stop because "I'll be there in thirty minutes," eventually became a knock never heard.

Sometimes he showed. And when he did, I didn't remem-ber a thing—a tear, a confused question of, "Where is Daddy at?" For now the answer was in the driver's seat, taking me somewhere unfamiliar (which didn't matter too much to me, as long as he was with me).

Looking at him, I loved his face most. His eyes had a won-derful darkness about them that, when stretched thin by his crooked smile, allowed me to see how I looked while laugh-ing. I could tell that his mind didn't sit still much. During the quiet times, when conversation couldn't hide the awkward-ness, he'd stare off with a conversation in his eyes that only he could hear.

Who I was made more sense when I was with him. He was a different mirror. With him, I could see where I'd gotten things my mama didn't own. I enjoyed every minute with this inconsistent relative I called "Daddy," until he started using words that I didn't believe belonged to him, like, "I love you." That sentence was too big to fit in his mouth. He even spit it out like he believed it when he said it—but I didn't. I couldn't. Love, as I'd understood it—through my mama—wasn't like the wind. Indifference was like that. Wind and indifference went wherever it pleased. Settling down when it benefited them, moving on without warning, even if it ripped a home or two apart on the way out. Love was like the sun—always there. It might've looked like it was moving—but it was forever still. Daddy couldn't stay put, so as far as I was concerned, Daddy didn't love me.

Over time, I was convinced. There can only be so many missed birthdays, missed first bike ride, missed changes in height, weight, grade, schools, until the heart becomes comfortable with keeping the man whose blood helped to build it, out.

———

I was old enough to listen well. Across from me, he leaned back on the porch chair, finishing a quick conversation with someone hanging half of their body out of the front door to reach him. The thin metal screen door swung back into place, clanging noisily as it did. Returning his chair back toward me.

"You know I love you, right?" I looked away. Not in an attempt to spare him from the way skepticism was redirecting my face, but to keep him from knowing that he could affect me at all.

"Yes . . ." I said.

"The way I am, I can love people and not really have to be around them. Like, I love you and all your siblings [he had two other children by his first wife]. I love my wife too [his third wife] but just the way I'm set up, if any of y'all ever wanted to stop speaking to me. Or just wanted to leave me alone, I wouldn't care. It doesn't mean I don't love you, it just wouldn't affect me."

I caught my mouth before it fell on the ground. Watching his features close, I read them to see if they could explain what his words said. Words had long become the secondary way for me to listen to people. People said what they didn't mean too much for me to believe that all words were real, but the body always added an unarticulated sentence, or two, to the dialogue.

Listening to his hands, he sounded relaxed. His voice, calm. It wasn't harsh; it was almost soft. His eyes, still very wonderful, were weightless. They didn't wander the ground; they kept their focus on me. From the looks of it, he was being nothing but honest, and it scared the vulnerability out of me. I couldn't understand how this man (my father) could tell me (his daughter) that any attempt at distancing myself from him would mean nothing. Do nothing. In fact, he would be able to continue his life, without me in it, as he'd been doing all along, with the steady peace of a man with no sins. This confession gave meaning to his method of fatherhood throughout the years. It obviously meant that he had the ability to love and not care, to come around, then not return. That he could sit across from someone with his same face and yet choose to never see them again. It proved that this man could not possibly love me. Or if he did, it was a sometimes love that my heart didn't have the capacity to hold. After that day, I would never call him again, and I doubt he noticed.

I learned how much of a risk trust is because of my father. That it couldn't be given away to a person just because they said they could have it. I'd see their palms open, fingers bent just slightly to make sure none could slip through the cracks, waiting on me to put my trust there. But it was mine. All mine. Folks can't take what they don't have access to. They could have my humor, share my food, know my address. Heck, they could even have some of my stories. I'd tell them just right, leaving out the crying parts, giving them just enough to think they knew me. I became unbothered and unfeeling because how else could I keep safe. But, at the same time that I was teaching myself how to avoid pain, I was also training myself to live without love.

> Love anything and your heart will be wrung and possibly broken. If you want to make sure of keeping it intact, you must give it to no one, not even an animal. Wrap it carefully round with hobbies and little luxuries; avoid all entanglements; lock it up safe in the casket or coffin of your selfishness. But in that casket—safe, dark, motionless, airless—it will change. It will not be broken; it will become unbreakable, impenetrable, irredeemable. . . . To love is to be vulnerable.[1]

I don't remember the different plot points that surrounded the occasion. Nor can I recall what I wore or what I ate for breakfast that morning. Was it a brown sweater or an orange T-shirt? Maybe it was waffles or possibly pancakes? I don't remember what my mother told me before she dropped me off at a family friend's home. One that she trusted to protect her baby until she came back from work. I'm sure she hugged me before saying goodbye, but who knows. It's all a blur until I remember the color of the basement.

---

[1] C. S. Lewis, *The Four Loves* (New York: Harcourt Brace, 1960), 121.

———

The basement was dark. The only light came through a small window in the corner. A couple of long beams of light sliced through the room, filling it with what looked like fog. How I ended up down there, only God knows. Being six or seven, the only reason I would've had for being told to go down there would've been for the promise of toys. Or games. Maybe hide-and-seek was what he—the teenage relative whose home I was in—wanted to play. Between the pool table, multiple closets, stacks of busted boxes, enclosed laundry room and the darkness itself, there were plenty of places to hide. I don't know how it all began—I only recall such a deep and undisturbed recognition that what he was doing to me didn't allow me to breathe normally. He told me to do it and I obeyed. Did it last fifty seconds or fifteen minutes? I don't know. He was bigger, older, and for all I knew, this too was a *game*.

A decade or so later, I paid particular attention to my TV when I heard a woman with wet eyes and a cracked-up voice tell Oprah about the molestation that occurred in her home. She described the soft violence that stole the innocent breath from her body. Her heart broke in front of the camera every time she remembered another detail. She'd close her eyes, turning her head left to right, trying to resist the clarity of her past. After each tear, her head got heavier. Putting words to the pain was an obvious weight she wasn't prepared to bear before an audience.

As I listened, I thought of the basement's darkness and what happened inside of it. What I heard and what I remembered sounded the same—except I'd never given it a name. To me, it was only something that happened to which I was too embarrassed to tell. According to this woman, I was a victim of sexual abuse. Having the ability to name what happened to me, released tears in both of my eyes. One fell, and several came after, until I found myself sharing not only this woman's story but also her grief. My head made a heavier sound, bending toward my chest, feeling my heart drop at the revelation of it being disregarded by the lusts of a teenage boy.

It's funny how, sometimes, the mind won't let the body remember what's been done to it. It chooses, at will, to take the abusive memory and bury it. As if to nurture away the pain by making us forget it's there. Not remembering trauma doesn't mean we're left without its effect. It still comes up and out, at a certain smell, sound, sight, touch, question, tone, location, person, people, personality. Waiting to be noticed and brought to the light. Letting it, and peeking into where it's from, is the path to making sense of ourselves and finding the particular healing we've been kept from having.

Between fatherlessness and sexual abuse, my entire frame of reference for people God made male was built on the experience of their doing. One man's absence taught me men were incapable of loving. Only in short, sporadic flashes of affection would they be able to do what they'd said they'd do. Made up of an inconsistent spine straightened out by everything else but their own flesh and blood, I refused to believe men could stand for truth, ever. The other man was not a real one at all, but while becoming a man, he decided to act out his urges on a child. A girl child whose first introduction to male affection wouldn't be her daddy's hug but another male's lusts. The consequence being that a man's touch sounded like everything unsafe. Sexual abuse, for me, turned male intimacy into an undignified practice of the male ego, to which I would only be a body to conquer and not a person to love.[2] I didn't know it with the same amount of assurance yet but all the while, another man was loving me, always.

---

[2] It is important to note that sexual abuse is not what made me gay. Nor did fatherlessness. They only exaggerated and helped direct the path for what was already there—which is sin (Psalm 51:5; Romans 1:26–27; James 1:15).

CHAPTER 5

2006

WE'D SINCE LEFT THE dance but what was asked followed me home. I couldn't get her question out of my head. "Jackie, you wanna be my girlfriend?" lingered between the ceiling and my collar bone, tethering itself to every thought, unhindered by any attempt of mine to set it free. When I told her, "No," the first time, she smiled and snatched her head back a bit, like I offended her or like she knew she was being lied to.

When I walked away, she stared and smirked toward my back, like she knew I'd eventually turn around and tell the truth—like she knew about second-grade, and the dreams that came even after I could spell. Even after I had a name for the flickering my heart made when a woman got close. She might've heard the straight words and saw right through the linear way in which they were said, into the constant craving to do what Leviticus called abominable. I'd heard more than one pastor say it, some even scream it, like the voice of someone trying not to swallow fire. But knowing that didn't keep me from wanting her, and it surely didn't make it any easier to admit, eventually to her, but first to myself.

———

I didn't want to go to hell. When I thought about her, I thought about *it*. I imagined what it would be like to live there, seeing the flames make use of my skin by turning it toward me, unclothed and fully insecure. I imagined wondering how not to be thirsty, when the heat snatched the air from my throat every time I opened it wide, to catch the fire's wind, hoping it could quench thirst. My nose would never hold the smell of espresso or flowers ever. Everything dead would be inhaled. Everything good would be gone and remembered as something taken for granted. I'd walk, forever fatigued, toward the end of the darkness praying for light, for hope, for a break, a breath, a hug, a smile turned toward me, a laugh, a prayer heard with the potential of being answered. God would hear but not speak. See but not rescue. Deliverance would be past tense, and the sermons I'd carried, but never believed, would be the ashes from which I ate. Hell would be a choice, and I had to decide if she was worth it.

This is what you've always wanted to do, I thought to myself. I'd only had dreams and long silent thoughts played out in broad daylight about being with women but I'd never had the courage to pursue it. The little moments of intimacy with women, such as a friend hugging me in the hallway or grabbing my arm during a short flash of laughter, always felt good and somewhat addictive. They'd only last long enough for me to know I wanted more and now I had the opportunity to have it. To grab the firefly by the wing before it gave its light to another sky.

"But what about hell?" That lightless place made up of people unable to like a different sex, would—according to the last church I sat in—be on the other side of choosing her. "I can just *try it* and see what's it's like." My heart and conscience were on opposite ends of a rope that I couldn't see, tugging at each end, waiting for me to decide who would fall.

Sitting in my bed, my conscience was as conversational as ever. I'd never known it to talk so much or maybe it did and I'd just gotten used to ignoring it. Plenty of times, it warned me of what not to smoke, or how much to drink, or what not to say or watch or meditate on—and not once had I listened. I did what I wanted to do. My conscience seemed to care more about the right thing than it did about what felt good and right *to me*.

My heart, on the other hand, knew me. It was the one that directed me from youth, leading me into brown plastic cabins. A couple of years later, at seven, while watching pornography at a friend's house, it told me to keep looking, to never tell, to remember all that I saw and to let it inside of my own house whenever my mother was asleep. Now, it just wanted me to be free. As free as the firefly once let go and released into the dark. There, surrounded by so much night, the blackness of it all made its body into a flame.

Through the walls, the room, the slow darkening of my conscience and the questions it asked that I was committed to ignoring, God looked. He could see what my mouth never said and hear what my heart whispered under its breath. It's the Eden delusion in which two fresh sinners take a tree as their covering (Genesis 3:8). Concluding that they can hide from the all-seeing God. Their sin, needing to be confessed is kept behind the bark, as if to find deliverance in its sap. God walks toward them, instead of runs, as if to announce that He is coming in the calmness of mercy. He asks them where they are. Not because He doesn't already know the answer but because He's giving them an opportunity to confess. To not only say where they are but *why* they are there. It's the denying of sin, the unwillingness to confess, the disregard for the completeness of God's knowledge of us and the fear it should elicit, that leaves no room for repentance. It is the deceived ones that think they can successfully hide from God.

Where shall I go from your Spirit?
Or where shall I flee from your presence?
If I ascend to heaven, you are there!

If I make my bed in Sheol, you are there!
If I take the wings of the morning
and dwell in the uttermost parts of the sea,
even there your hand shall lead me,
and your right hand shall hold me.
If I say, "Surely the darkness shall cover me,
and the light about me be night,"
even the darkness is not dark to you;
the night is bright as the day,
for darkness is as light with you. (Psalm 139:7–12)

My secret was no secret at all. My sins were all ever before Him. And my conscience was that cool-of-the-day, garden-type of walk telling me that there was nowhere to hide. God was listening and ready to whisper back in a different voice. A true voice that says, "If we confess our sins, he is faithful and just to forgive us our sins and to cleanse us from all unrighteousness" (1 John 1:9). But I didn't want Him to hear and forgive. I would only listen to the voices that led me away from the light. I wanted the freedom that was hidden in the dark.

I'd heard Christians talk about freedom and how it happened to them only when God got ahold of their heart and stripped the hardness clean off. That way, they could do unnatural things like "obey" and "trust His Word." Statements when told to me, a lover of disobedience, sounded as silly as slavery.

Being honest with myself, I knew that I wanted to be gay with her. Having access to her only through social media gave me the opportunity to tell her the truth without me having to see what it did to her face. If, when she read my message, the smirk returned and bloomed into the smile of one who'd been proven right. When she responded, I read it and felt weightless. As if the roof above me cracked open and I flew, hitting my ankle against the freshly split edge on the way out. This was more for me than her. This was my way of exploring the world and my place in it. She was only the fuel. I needed her to tell my legs how the sky carried weight. How up there, walking doesn't work. That flying doesn't involve your arms or legs at all. You only need to let go and watch how quickly the night sky will take you with it. Ever so often, my mouth would open and the darkness would brush against my teeth and end up spreading around my tongue. Who knew freedom felt like this?

Closing the door behind me, I guided her toward the back of the house only with my voice. Without fear of my lingering gaze being caught, I watched her walk in front of me. Toward the back of my mother's house (she was at work at the time) was a sunroom. Plants she'd named after people she never met filled up the space and turned it green. I sat down next to "Lavinia" and heard the flick of a lighter. It took a few times for the flame to climb out and meet its match but when it did, the room slowly started to look like something more than a blunt was being burned in it. Smoke spread into each corner, turning the sunroom into a foggy version of the moon. After inhaling a little of it for herself, she passed it to me to smoke. I inhaled the night and exhaled a request, "Sit down."

We sat, high and mighty in the cloudy room, comfortable in each other's space for as long as the twisted blunt could be held. Our closeness was unlike how preachers had described it. They said it was unnatural. Sometimes, following it up with a clever rhyme about how God made "Adam and Eve, not Adam and Steve." But for me, their little silly psalm didn't change how good it felt to be near her. What they called strange felt more natural to me than heterosexuality had ever been. Her entire body made me feel at home in myself. I held her tighter, not wanting it all to fade into a dream again, where I was only gay in my sleep.

She found me looking at her from over her shoulder and smiled. This time, it had a little bit of surprise in it. Like watching a firefly light up more of the sky than you expected it to. "What?" I asked her. She was obviously learning something about me, and I wanted her to say it out loud. "Clearly, you've always been gay." I looked up at her girlish eyes, and smirked.

CHAPTER 6

2007

YOU SHOULD DRESS LIKE a stud tonight," my new girl-friend said, crossing her sunlit legs, while sitting on top of my bed. A few months had passed since I'd been with the woman that turned me out into the world where women kissed each other and liked it. In this community, gay black folk, I'd soon learn, had a different language amongst themselves than that of the straight world around them.

What straight people called a regular-looking girl—those that wore purses, nails, lip gloss, heels, dresses, skirts, and talked as if she had a boyfriend instead of a girlfriend—we called "fem." Tomboy had long described the likes of me—the type of girl that hated purses, dresses, lip gloss, skirts, and always talked a little more aggressive than how everyone said a girl should speak. But in this newfound environment where the rainbow was always visible, even when the sun wasn't, tomboys were typically given a new name: stud. In my relationship, the stud role was already how I behaved. I opened doors, paid for meals, protected when necessary, led always, was held by the waist never, I bent down only when she needed to hold my neck as we hugged, and I'd pull her in just to remind her that I was stronger. And now, she wanted me to dress how I spoke, and allow all of the "masculinity" to reflect in what I put on.

I borrowed some blue jeans from a male friend that lived five houses down from my own. I slid one leg in and what felt like electricity darted between my left leg and the inseam. It stopped once it reached my face and became a smile. I laughed, only to keep the excitement controlled. The other pant leg went on just as easy, the same electric sensation shot through my right leg, it went around my knee, past my torso and underneath the oversized red long-sleeve shirt, until it made its way into my hands. I pulled the pants up toward my waist, letting them relax a little, creating a small sag, just like the men I knew would do.

It didn't help that I wasn't considered girly enough for the world. When age took ahold, I distanced myself from what some considered feminine. Pink was ugly, so I didn't wear it. Dresses were awkward, so I didn't put them on. Purses were inconvenient, so I didn't hold them. These things were, to them, what made girls *girls*. It didn't matter that in us girls, were the third to last letters in the alphabet that told our bodies to spread our hips out wide one day to prepare our bodies for holding life. Or that in us, was not the instinct to jump in front of a bullet for a man but to be the first warm face he saw once he fell to the ground. Holding his head and hand, with a voice that had no apple from Adam to make it heavy, telling him "It'll be okay." It didn't matter that our frame carried more meat than muscle, more nurture than anything, or that our chests grew out and became what no boy gained during puberty. It didn't matter that we all laughed in shame that time we weren't prepared to bleed during school—we didn't ask the boys how it felt the first time they got their period. Why would we? They were boys. Boys only bled from playing too much and fighting too hard. We bled by nature. Nature as it was shown in my body called me "Woman."

But society called me manly. They'd made women out to be people who wear their legs out and men to be those that spoke as if everyone should listen. Neither versions were a sufficient mirror. I'd need someone smarter and not created to tell me who I was, for He would be the one who'd know best.

———

For all we know, identity and the concept of goodness came into this world together. When God made Adam and Eve, He first made them in His image. He wanted them to be different than the stars, plants, and animals. They wouldn't exist like the other created things, being both beautiful and soulless.

They'd be able to reflect God on Earth, in body, mind, and soul. Being an image-bearer was their primary identity. It would have them tell the world, by living, for whom and for what reason they were made. At the same time, they were also made distinctly different from one another.

God made them male and female[3]—two words not crafted by a person, or group, or society, or culture, or America for that matter, but used by God to describe what He'd made and exactly what He'd designed them to be. Out of the same God came two different bodies. And after creating them, lastly, after all that had been made before, God looked at them and everything else and called it and them good. The plants? Good. The stars? Good. The fish's fins? Good. What about Adam and Eve? What about their eyes, and how their mind made them see the same thing through a different lens? Or their hands, and how Adam's were wide enough to hold a hoof or two and Eve's small enough to fit a bird in it. Or Eve's voice and how it sounded like morning and his, sounding like he'd just spit out a mountain. Or his brow bone, strong as a fist. Her face, soft as an amen. All of this, God said was a *very good* thing. Why? Because a good God made it.

Sin hates everything good and when Adam and Eve decided to live in it, something interesting happened. They

---

[3] Genesis 5:2.

ate the fruit, sinning against God, their eyes opened, and the first thing they noticed was their body. They were naked, and now they knew it. Nothing had changed yet everything had changed. Both bodies were the same as they were before they believed the devil, but now sin played a part in how they saw themselves. What was beautiful before was now an object of shame, reminding them of their broken relationship with God, and each other.

The same way that sin had taken my affections for its own bidding, being born craving, delighting in all things unnatural, it had both hands wrapped around my mind as well. Turning it in on me, like an inverted scope, unable to see honestly, only dimly. Where the body I lived in felt like I'd been given the wrong clothing. Another shirt looked better, warmer, easier to put on. Mine, stranger, uncomfortable, itchy, and impossible to take off. If I were able to see God's goodness in all that He'd made, including me and my woman-ness, then I would've easily understood that my body was not left out from the words of Colossians 1:16: "For by him all things were created, in heaven and on earth, visible and invisible, whether thrones or dominions or rulers or authorities—*all things were created through him and for him*." My hands, head, face, legs, hips, hormones, private parts, voice, feet, fingers, feelings, were all made by Him and *for* Him. Apparently, this body was never mine to begin with—it was *given* to me from Somebody, for Somebody. Somebody who'd made it for glory and not shame. Until I got to know Him though, my identity would be made up of whatever dust that flew up from the devil's feet as he ran through the earth.

———

Every weekend, we were there. Knowing it was the only place we could sleep next to each other with no concern for who might walk into the bedroom. We walked into the hotel lobby, her hand resting on my forearm. Nobody was at the check-in counter, so we sat down and waited. We'd been together almost six months, but time didn't matter when we touched. Taller than me but as beautiful as a newborn butterfly, I'd met her through a friend. At first, we only talked a text at a time. I had a girlfriend already, for close to a year and a half, but I wanted a new laugh to listen to occasionally. After my ex-girlfriend suggested I become a stud, and I listened, women flew and flocked to my every move. I guess my face looked better under a brim. Each one of them said things I'd never heard about myself. Mainly, that I was wanted.

They lusted after me. I loved *it*, never *them*. Except two: the one that helped me out of my cocoon and the other sitting next to me.

The door swung open and smashed the wall behind it, cracking the wallpaper just enough to hear it break. I saw his back before his face. He moved through the door and behind the front desk like a 6-foot-4 tornado, spinning with gravel skin, eyes switching places with the left and right walls, looking for something or someone to lift off the ground. As soon as he entered, he left into another room. Whoever he was looking for, wasn't in the lobby, or behind the desk, or outside.

My girlfriend threw her eyes at me. They weren't as light as they were before the wrath-bent man tore through the lobby. She said nothing and everything at the same time. Between her blinks, I heard "I'm scared, of him, of this. Will you protect me when he comes back? If he comes back, can you catch him so I can go free?" I told her "no" without saying a word. Hearing him boom his mountain-ness voice through the walls, remembering his arms, while looking at mine, I felt like a woman. What her eyes said, I said too.

I wanted to turn toward someone full of testosterone and beg him to be strong for us. To gather up all the stuff God gave him for a time such as this and protect us. I couldn't protect her, or me. And I knew it. Knowing it irked me, quietly. It was such an inconvenient time for my conscience to remind me of reality. Why couldn't it just let me keep eating dust and calling it food? These clothes, these women, these dreams, this voice, her submission to it, this heavy walk that made my mother cringe, weren't they the truth? Didn't they mean I had successfully transformed? Couldn't I be what I wanted to be? Between me and God, in the secrecy of my conscience, my being a woman felt inescapably real. As much as I'd believed I could, when in the presence of a man made to be one, I knew there was a natural distinction between the two of us that even the heaviness of my voice couldn't undo. In the other room, his voice still shook the walls. The louder it got, the more I remembered my first name.

CHAPTER 7

2007

I ALWAYS WONDERED IF she knew I was gay. I tried, as best as I could, to treat my girl like a plain friend in front of her. Even when I wanted to hold my girlfriend's hand, or stare long and lustfully, or watch her move across the room, I had to bury it all until we were alone. Anybody that knew what intimacy looked like would've smelled it on us. We sat too close for it to be an accident. In front of parents, our hugs looked staged. We smiled differently, lovingly, inside of conversations that didn't deserve it. Before the edges of our mouths curled back down, they tarried first. Catching ourselves, we'd turn our heads away quickly, like two children caught in an act of disobedience. But my mother still saw it. She saw it all.

I hated talk radio but it helped her enter the day well. Both of us, mother and daughter, boss and employee (I worked with her at the same restaurant she'd met my father at eighteen years prior), rode to work together weekday mornings. This morning in particular glared like a Wednesday with Monday's burdens. The disc jockey talked, and talked, and talked about nothing that mattered to me. Out of the window, each house blurred as we drove past them. A welcome distraction from the annoying voice inside of the car, coming from the speakers, making my mother say, "hmm" and "uh huh."

A different voice was coming out of the speakers now. She'd been speaking for what might've been a minute, about what? I didn't know, but catching the end of her monologue, I figured she was speaking anecdotally.

She was describing how this person dressed, how it was the first sign. Then how this person had a friend that came to her house, leaving only to come back when school was out the next day. How this person and their friend's interactions were strange, noticeable, so much so that her left eyebrow raised every time this friend came around this person.

"Did you talk to your daughter about the stuff you were noticing?" the disc jockey interrupted. "I did. I brought it up, and she denied it. Said 'Mama, that's just my friend.' But I ain't believe her. I knew what she was, I was just waitin' on her to tell me."

Still looking out of the window, as not to make it obvious that the radio had my full attention, I listened, reluctantly, to this woman describe her daughter. Her daughter sounded like me (dressed like me too). Her daughter's friend sounded like my girl. Even the way this mother talked about the way she looked at them when they were all in the same room flashed me back to the suspicion my own mother's mouth carried when around me and my girlfriend. The disc jockey interrupted again, "Well thank you for joining us! Alright now, we got parents calling in to answer the question, 'How did you know your child was gay?' Next caller . . ."

My mother turned the volume up.

One more guest talked about me without using my name before the volume faded into silence. My mother parked the car. I gulped and looked out of the window again, this time, to quiet the tears.

"Is that you?" she said. She sounded sure of what the answer would be and sad at having to ask for it.

"Yes." It was a broken yes but an honest one. Strangely enough, once said, nothing but grief took a breath.

My mother looked outside, gathering strength from the trees. "I knew it," she said. And I knew she did. I just didn't want to tell her the truth from my own mouth until I was out from under her roof. Next to the hallway, inside of my room, in front of the bed, in between the walls, I planned to live closeted.

All of my friends knew and loved me still. I was never afraid of their faces, and if they would become a back turned on me after I admitted to them who I was. Their acceptance was easy to come by—a common currency friends sold and purchased before the bell rang. But the closet door was swung open by another's hand. A voice, a description, a perfectly timed segment that spoke on my behalf.

Her face was what I didn't want to see. I thought telling her I was somebody's daughter's girlfriend would turn it black. I figured she'd feel betrayed. I could see her imagining my wedding—her sitting in the front row, a man and me, standing on an altar, burned into a myth. And children? Oh, children. I saw her weep at not getting to see my stomach grow. If my girlfriend carried for us both, how gray it would make her. Seeing her daughter behave like a father would inevitably shatter all dreams of normalcy. I didn't want to see the disappointment, or hear it made into words. But I did. I couldn't avoid hearing her exhale heavy, before saying, "I love you, we will talk about this later."

I didn't want to talk. Talking is what started all of this.

———

Being "out" felt better than I thought it would. Closets were made for clothes, not people. On the outside, I could breathe louder, standing next to my girl with my hand around her waist in public. Being watched like lights in a room, after a while, became a tradition. Mothers, fathers, children, grandparents, straight men, straight girls, store clerks, cops, folks on the bus, folks walking—everybody stared at us. Saint Louis, being not too far removed from the Southern culture of holiness or hell, passed down through each watcher's bloodline, must have made them think that making a terrible face would make me pick up a Bible. If not that, they looked because they couldn't help it. *How strange*, they thought, *two women in love*.

Depending on the neighborhood, we'd run into grins—the same kind of grins you saw lined up alongside the summer's pride parade. And man, did they feel good. With their cheeks touching the bottom lobe of each ear, you could taste the inclusivity of their affection, and the boldness of their approval. They stared too, but it was no different than how strangers look at two lovebirds using their wings to embrace. They watched to take part in the love, not to condemn it. Becoming forgetful, what I knew the Bible said about us was less important around them. Their glee contradicted my conscience to the point of confusion. Confusion as to how God could dislike what made a good number of both straight and gay folk smile. As much as I wanted to believe God grinned when He thought of my life, I knew He didn't.

My conscience spoke to me throughout the day. In the morning, it reminded me of God. A few minutes before the clock brought the noon in, it brought God to mind, again. Night was when it was the loudest. On the way to sleep, my head lay relaxed on my pillow surrounded by the natural darkness of night, I thought about God. If being intrigued by Scripture and reading it to cure boredom had done anything, it had made me aware of a truth about me and Him that I couldn't shake even if the earth moved. I was *His* enemy (James 4:4). How could I, an enemy of God, have sweet dreams knowing that He sat awake throughout the night?

Letting my mind wander in the other direction, I recalled love and how He was *it*. When it sounded like He was using my conscience to speak, I remembered Jesus. I thought about His hands, gesturing sinners to come. Waving each back and forth, continuously, unhesitatingly, as if with each time, He was saying "Come. Please come. Where else can you go to find life except through Me? Come all sinners, come." It was maddening to try and sleep with so much noise in the room.

Keisha was a Christian, and my cousin. I had the numbers of very few Christians in my phone, and even fewer that I could call and have a conversation with that didn't end up as a one-sided dialogue on the book of Leviticus. God was haunting me. Keisha knew Him already, so my hope was that she could help me understand why. He knew I was gay, and she did too. So why was He talking to *me* so much? And what did I have to do to quiet Him down.

"Keisha . . . I feel like God is callin' me."

"Okay." I felt her nod her head. "Why do you think that?"

"Cuz . . . idk . . . it's like it just feels like it. Like, whatever I do, I can sense God trying to get my attention. Like, even when I'm being myself, I can feel how wrong it is."

"Mmhmm."

"But the thing is, I don't want God. Like, I really don't."

She'd known me since I'd come out of the womb, and was more than a decade older than me. She took a breath, a deep "God use me" kind of breath and said, "I've been praying for you. When you told me you were gay, I blamed myself. Said 'God, could I have been in her life more?' I thought it *had* to be something I did wrong. But God told me just pray."

I said nothing, not wanting to disrupt her train of honest thought. "Then God told me to give you to Him, to not worry about it. But I told God how much I loved you, cuz, I didn't know how to just let this go, and you know what He told me?" She laughed a little, like she was setting me up for the punch line of a joke. "He told me 'I love her more than you do.' And since then, I've just been praying." She chuckled again, like she knew something I didn't. "I'm not worried about you, Jackie. God's hand is on you and He's going to do what He has to do to show you how much you need Him."

After the conversation was ended with a prayer, I hung up even more confused than I was before she answered the phone. *God is going to show me how much I need Him? He loves me more than she does? What does that even mean?* I thought. The only thing that made sense was that someone had obviously been talking to God about me and it was the reason why God wouldn't leave me alone. Obviously, whatever was being asked of Him, regarding me, was making my little sinful world spin. It was dizzying to live on now-a-days. Trying to stand up straight (or should I say, queer), made everything I loved, mainly myself and my girlfriend, blurry. Nothing was clear except God's loud voice saying, "Come."

I started smoking more than usual because it kept God away. The thick dancing smoke would fill up my body and silence the war, the truth, the Scriptures, the hands of Christ, especially when they bled, stretched and still welcoming sinners, including the one dying next to Him. Unless His hands could take my own, lifting them toward heaven, signaling a surrender of the will, I would not give Him anything except resistance.

———

"Sorry about your dad." The text message simple, precise, sent by a friend who'd found out before I did, unaware that her condolences were what broke the news. I stared at the screen, while reading its words, begging my eyes to interpret them differently, my heart stilled. "What do you mean?" My reply was genuine. This "sorry" could've been an apology for many things: Maybe she'd heard of the distance between me and my father and felt sorry for it. Or of the last time we'd spoken, when he mentioned how he noticed that "Daddy" was never the name I used to address him. No names were used at all. No affectionate pronoun was fitting to describe how he'd been to me. I skipped the dishonest words, such as Dad, Daddy, Father, Pop, and went straight to the subject of what needed to be said, making sure to look him in his eyes so that he'd know who I was speaking to. Was she apologizing for the graduation he lived fifteen minutes away from and never attended? Or that I only remembered him smiling through the smoke of one blown-out candle in eighteen birthdays? A year had gone between us. Since seeing that crooked smile, broken brow, and hard-headed voice that I'd gotten all of my intelligent rebellion from. But she didn't know anything about the past year or years. She only knew what I didn't want to believe. My father was gone, forever this time.

The news was shocking. Something in me had always hoped for the day he'd love me always instead of sometimes. I walked into my room, laid on my bed, and put my tears into the pillow. It's not as if I wasn't used to his absence, I just didn't know how to get used to the permanence of it. Even when we skipped a few years at a time, there would still be the rare phone call, the resumed conversation, even if I couldn't see it, the knowledge that he was breathing somewhere muted the intensity of my daily grief.

Most likely because of how infrequent it was to see him, once gone forever, I didn't miss my father. It would probably take much more effort to miss someone that was never around. But yet, I still continued to grieve the death of hope. Any chance of me calling him "Daddy" was now dead. Life resumed as usual after the funeral. There, I was reminded of how unknown I was to the people who knew him better than I. Despite our same eyes, more than once, I was asked, "Who are you in relation to Jeff?" to which I would tell them a fact they obviously needed a eulogy to discover. "I'm his daughter," I'd say. Smiling awkwardly with his same face brought back to life. When the burial concluded and the days after grew tall enough for me to see, it brought to my life some self-inflicted and strangely unexpected difficulty. After losing my father, me and my mother's relationship dwindled away by my being unbelievably disrespectful. She might've been my mother by name, but she was nothing more than another source of authority to dismiss. Home got harder, less time could be spent there, more money was tossed into weed-scented pockets, a few hours in a cell came from helping friends put on clothes they didn't buy. One night after my car, bought a month prior, was towed a block from my girlfriend's house, I stood on her porch with a friend. Passing the blunt between us, I shook my head at what seemed to be Keisha's "encouragement" coming to life. "Is God trying to get my attention by making my life harder or something?" I said. Blowing out smoke between questions, said out loud but mainly meant for God to hear and relent. "I mean, does God want me *that* much?"

As grace would have it, He did.

CHAPTER 8

2008

THE TV WAS ON. Sobriety was an unwelcome guest. The night before, my girlfriend and I laid up with all of the weed I bought for the week and smoked it all away. Because of our impulsiveness, tonight was free from smoke and my mind was without distraction. Laying on the bed, my left hand held my phone, my right side burrowed into the warm side of the mattress, my right hand cradling the pillow deaf ear. Thoughts woke up between commercials, with nothing important to say.

"What time do I even have to work tomorrow?"

"Ima have to call ol girl to give me a ride."

"I wonder how her mama doing."

"My mama prolly still mad at me for coming home high."

"Where's the remote? Ima see what else is on."

"She will be the death of you."

I sat up quick, like I'd seen a ghost or felt a hand on my back. The thought wasn't audible but loud enough to interrupt everything. All other conversations within me quieted down and my heart got heavy as a brick. Where the sentence came from, I didn't know. I couldn't map its origins.

"Was it the devil?"

"Nah, I don't think I'd feel convicted if it was the devil."

"Maybe it was just me."

"It couldn't have been just *me*."

"But it's in my mind so it has to be me."

"But I didn't think that up . . . it just CAME."

"Or maybe it was God."

I figured only God would say such a thing. Like a flashing red light, He was trying to warn me. Warn me of death. A death, supposedly soon to come because of who I loved. I loved a woman, to death, apparently. Was He saying this because He wanted me to choose? Choose what would give me life instead? He was life, or at least that's what the preacher once said. If that were the case, then did He want me to choose *Him*? To choose Him would mean I had to leave her. This didn't sound like a fair transaction. In my mind, choosing God was the same as choosing heterosexuality. It would become a holy mandate.

Such as sobriety is to a born-again alcoholic, I thought, and who wants to live like that. Being in a relationship with a man, in the name of God?

I know now what I didn't know then. God was not calling me to be straight; He was calling me to Himself. The choice to lay aside sin and take hold of holiness was not synonymous with heterosexuality. From my prior understanding of God as told by the few Christians I'd met, to choose God would be to inevitably choose men too. Even if my liking of them became a way for me to chase away the gayness without God's help, I figured, that's what would please Him most. That when He looked at me, He saw a wife before He saw a disciple. But God was not a Las Vegas chaplain or an impatient mother, intent on sending a man my way to "cure" me of my homosexuality. He was God. A God after my whole heart, desperate to make it new. Committed to making it like Him. In my becoming Holy as He is, I would not be miraculously made into a woman that didn't like women; I'd be made into a woman that loved God more than anything. If marriage ever came[4] or singleness called me by name, He wanted to guarantee by the work of His hands that both would be lived unto Him. (To my surprise, years later, marriage did come. But in God calling me, it was not for me

---

[4] For further reading on this, see "Same-Sex Attraction and the Heterosexual Gospel" on page 177 later in this book.

to find a man to love. Or to live as if my same-sex attractions weren't a reality; it was to love God with all my heart, mind, and soul [Matthew 22:36–37].)

The thought of death was so matter-of-fact that it made an immediate mess of my mind. Like God had thrown Himself inside of my world, in one immediate gesture, while I watched everything shred, fly up, and rain down all at once. My conscience was bearing witness to the truth, and I could no longer deny it. It would've been a waste of time. Time that I knew did not belong to me. This death was nearer to me than my skin. The preacher, between short tenor riffs, told our congregation, that the wages of sin was death. Remembering this, I considered, "Hadn't I been dead for a long time now?"

I'd been sinning my entire life. But I was not alive—I was only breathing. And God wanted me to believe it before even that passed away. I knew He required me to let go of my girlfriend specifically, but more than her came to mind.[5] *What else was I loving that might be the death of me?* I wondered. There had to be more executioners that I'd made my lover. While thinking, more sins came to mind. How easy it is to recall your sins when you realize you've already been sentenced. Like bottled confetti cracked open and spread across the ceiling—pride,

---

[5] For further reading on the biblical view of same sex relationships: *What Does the Bible Really Teach about Homosexuality?* by Kevin DeYoung.

lust, pornography, lying, dishonoring authority, and lesbianism fell face-first (all of them being the more obvious sins). They wore loud clothes and shiny shoes. But each of them stemmed from one root—one organic sin that grew up, branched out, and became the seeded fruit of all other sins.

Unbelief: it was from this sin from which I hung, guilty as charged.

I'd never gotten around to changing the channel. The TV's commotion went on unnoticed as the room had now become too surreal to recognize. I didn't know what to call this moment. Surrender, to me, had never been explained in these terms. There were no pews nearby, with emotive-laden music to woo me from my seat. No preacher howling Scriptures through a cordless mic, with his left arm gesturing for this sinner to "come." Beneath me wasn't an aisle leading to an altar for me to lay my sins. All of my many, many sins probably wouldn't have had enough room on a common altar anyway. It was only me, my room, and God.

Not more than twenty-four hours before, me and my girlfriend laid our burdens where our hearts were kept. I knew of no better sanctuary to feel safe with. Both her eyes were stained glass windows that carried the sunlight in. She made my days bright.

She was an answered prayer that God forbid me to speak. I loved her, but according to God, our love was no different than death. Why would God want to keep me from this, I thought again—wasn't He love? Shouldn't He understand it best? Especially the ways in which it made all of His creatures feel a little more like Him every time they were *in* it.

On the other hand, if He was love, the embodiment of it without the slightest wrinkle in His robe, what love is when devils cannot interfere—then all other loves must've been a lesser love at best. Could it be that God would not have me going about the rest of my life believing that these lesser forms of "love" were the real thing?

Perhaps this love He, filled to the brim with, was pouring over into His dealings with me. And perhaps this love was compelling Him, on the basis of grace—an undeserved love—to help me see that every person, place, or thing that I loved more than Him could not keep its promise to love me eternally. Nor was my heart created for them to hold. But they would instead do to me what all sin does, separate me from God, and thus true love, forever. It would be the death of me.

Allowing my sexuality to rule me was a death sentence, but so was everything else. Before tonight, I wouldn't have called myself self-righteous. The common church crowd, with their raised noses, and long skirts, prancing around like they were born saved, sanctified, and filled with the Holy Ghost, were the ones who fit that description, not me. They were the ones that forgot that their rags were filthy even if their clothes were clean. They'd lost memory of how God couldn't be bribed with good works and big hats. Heaven only opened its gates for those Jesus escorted in, but they were the kind of folk that invited themselves and called it righteousness.

But, I—unbeknownst to me—had been swayed by this same leaven. If only I could just be straight, and lay aside my homosexuality, God would accept me and call me His own, I used to think. This delusion was the belief that only one aspect of my life was worthy of judgment, while the rest deserved heaven. That my other vices were "not as bad." They were just struggles that I had to work on instead of repenting.

There is a possibility that this kind of self-righteous thinking is why salvation has eluded many same-sex-attracted men and women. You will hear them say how they've sought God's help in this matter. They have asked Him to make them straight and He has, according to them, denied them access to the miraculous. Because God did not take hold of their gay desires and replace them with straight desires, they have no other choice but to follow where their affections may lead. The error is this: they have come to God believing that only a fraction of themselves needs saving. They have therefore neglected to acknowledge the rest of them also needs to be made right. It is like coming to God offering only a portion of their heart for Him to have, as if He does not have the right to take hold of it all or as if what has been withheld from Him can be satisfied without Him.

A thorough survey of my own heart, led entirely by the Holy Spirit, allowed me to see what I'd never seen: that I not only needed freedom from homosexuality, but from all sin. I was holistically in need of God. But even still, I didn't know Him too well. Didn't know if when I laid my heart bare before Him, and emptied its contents of every form of safety and love I'd ever known, if He would be large enough to fill it up again. I knew that He'd fill it with Himself; He was too jealous of a God not to do so. But would all that He is be enough? What He called idols had been a kind of joy for me. In Him, would I find a better one? Or perhaps, would He not merely give me joy but would He *be* my joy?

I hadn't yet moved from my spot in the bed. Something holy was happening here, now. The God who made light to shine in the darkness was now doing this work in me. This work of breaking into and overcoming the blindness I was born embracing. Jesus started making sense. I mean, He is God.

The Jesus my Sunday school teachers told me about could walk on water. Could make man out of dust and used dirt to unveil darkened eyes. Angels worshiped Him. Satan couldn't defeat Him. He'd always been alive. At no point in forever had He ever needed another to be His full self. Nothing could be compared to Him, in heaven or on the earth. Everything good came from Him.

In Him, being good and holy and merciful and jealous and wise and perfect and love and incomprehensible and triune and amazing and magnificent and beautiful and grand and insanely wonderful, how could I ever glory in a created thing when it was made of the same substance that formed all that I am? How could I live for something that was made as if it would not return from whence it came but He, God in Christ, came from heaven for *me*, of all people.

Who gave mercy my address? Or told it how to get to my room? Didn't it know a sinner lived in it? On the way down the hall, shouldn't the smell of idols kept its feet from moving any closer. Then I remembered the one verse of the Bible that I knew by heart. "For God so loved the world that He gave His only Son, that whoever believes in Him shall not perish but have eternal life."

The same Bible that condemned me held in it the promises that could save me. I just had to believe it. "It" being what it said about Him: God. Jesus had the guilty in mind when He was hung high and stretched out wide. On it, He died in my place, for my sin. He, bare-bodied and face set on joy, became as a slaughtered lamb underneath the wrath of God. You would think His Father would have a better memory than that. Didn't He know that that wrath was mine? It even had my name on it. But He knew. His justice wouldn't allow Him to forget. His love is what He wanted me to know and remember, and I did.

"What You are calling me to do, I can't do it on my own, but I know enough about You to know that You will help me," I said to God, my new friend. I didn't know that the confession of my inability to please Him and the shifting of my back away from the sins I'd previously embraced was repentance. Nor did I recognize that my resolve to believe that He could be to me what no one else could, was faith. But it was. Without asking me my permission, a good God had come to my rescue.

PART 2

Who I Became

CHAPTER 9

2008

I ARRIVED AT WORK the next day, a new creature. Though my soul was much different, my clothes were the same. My extra-large uniform, with its dark blue button-up and oversized black Dickies didn't feel normal anymore. My best friend and coworker Mike looked at me and said, "You look different." "What you mean?" I said, considering the fact that my boxers were still showing and my chest was flattened by an extra small sports bra. "I don't know, man. You just look, brighter." Maybe he noticed that the veil had been removed but didn't know what to call it.[6]

It felt weird to enter back into the world after meeting God. Just two days ago, I was flirting with girls during my lunch break. But now I knew God was watching. It was not as if He hadn't seen me before; the difference was, I actually cared.

---

[6] 2 Corinthians 3:16.

A little after our lunch rush, when the hordes of 9-to-5ers-turned-mob finally went back to their cubicles, I was told to transition from food prep to the cash register. Working the register put you up close and personal with the people—everything an introvert like me would give anything to avoid. While doing small talk with a customer who had more questions than I had the patience for, I noticed a girl standing in line. She was beautiful. If it were any other day, I would've stared in her direction long enough for her to notice. Even if she wasn't gay, I was always confident that I could be all of the motivation she needed. If she stared back with a smile, it would be her way of telling me the truth about herself without saying one word. But today, I couldn't stare. Well, I could. Salvation didn't disable my eyes from functioning, nor her beauty from disrupting the room. I could've, without question, done what I'd always done, allow this body to rule me. In it sat another master, however—One who was involved with an empty tomb and a risen Savior.

———

See, after Jesus was crucified, His body was placed in the tomb of a rich man who had not yet died. The obvious conclusion by anyone who knew the permanence of death would be that Jesus' body would be there forever. Or at least until it became dust and collapsed in on itself from decomposition. But, in typical fashion, God did what He said He would do. Resurrect. When a few of Jesus' followers went to Jesus' grave some days after He had been laid there, they were shocked to see Him not in it. He had *just* been there. He was dead. Dead things don't disappear. Unless, the dead body is no longer that but alive as it had been before. But that would mean that something or someone greater than death was there to help.

Death was the Goliath no stone could defeat and the Red Sea no staff could part. God had spoken about its arrival being the proper and inevitable consequence of sin. From the long-lived yet still-dead body of Adam to the headless death of he who had unworthy hands and a voice crying in the wilderness, death reigned. Until God came. Three days after Christ laid His life down, He got up, literally. The nuisance death had become for everyone dead or alive was now defeated. And Jesus, not being one to leave a dirty space to itself, gathered up the linen that once laid on His face, folded it, then placed it on the surface that once held His body. Maybe this was a metaphor. All who would enter the tomb might see that Jesus never leaves any place the same way it was when He entered it.

Sometime later, Jesus appeared to His disciples in bodily form. For there is no such thing as a resurrection that does not include the body. After showing them His hands and His feet to prove that He was Him fully, with flesh and bone,

He tells them, "And behold, I am sending the promise of my Father upon you. But stay in the city until you are clothed with power from on high" (Luke 24:49). The promise and the power were the same. Jesus had promised to not leave His disciples as orphans, but He would instead send the third person of the Godhead, the Holy Spirit. Once the Holy Spirit came, they would then receive power. The same power that moved into Jesus' tomb and untangled each limb from death's cords. Making sure not to neglect the heart and the brain, the quiet organs began to play again with a new song and the skin reversed and returned to its previous color. Muscles and bone regathered their strength and followed the Spirit's lead, out and into life. What human being has seen a power such as this? Granted, we have been made privy to other forms of power. Such as when we see the same sun rise day after day, and year and year without the slightest hint that it may one day fall. Or when we have taken pleasure in seeing the ocean turn in on itself, and wondered, *What in the world is keeping it from turning in on me?* How is it that water, a mindless substance, knows submission better than I. Or gravity. The kind of power that has kept us all from becoming wingless birds unable to land. These earthly demonstrations of power have a heavenly source, God (Colossians 1:17). And God, through Christ, had given this same power, to me.

She was still in line. The talkative guy had since left but there were a few customers between her and me. I was trying to pay attention to what the person before me was ordering, but I kept noticing her smile behind them. And at the same time, I sensed in me a conflict of interest. There she was, as pretty as she can be. Surely I could get her if I wanted to—and I *wanted* to.

But I also wanted something else: God. In me was this strange conviction that there was another route He wanted me to go, another beauty He made for me to delight in and I didn't know what to do with myself. I'd been His child for less than twenty-four hours and He was already changing me. *Is this what it feels like to be a Christian?* I thought to myself. *Is it to have a quiet war inside of yourself at all times?*

Wanting God over a woman was an entirely new experience for me. It wasn't even something I'd considered as being a part of Christianity, let alone the Christian. It seemed to be a religion of *just* duty. I'd met so many disciples who preached more of sin than joy, whose eyes were stuck in a constant state of solemnity, clenched teeth and an endless fascination with holiness. Why hadn't they ever mentioned the place happiness had within righteousness, or how the taking up of the cross would be a practice of obtaining delight? Delight in all that God is? Even their Savior had this kind of joy in mind as He endured His cross. So why hadn't they set their focus on the same? In their defense, they were not to blame for my unbelief. I just wonder if they would've told me about the beauty of God just as much, if not more, than they told me about the horridness of hell, if I would've burned my idols at a faster pace.

I was able to *want* God because the Holy Spirit was after my affections just as much as He was after my obedience. The tenant that had previously occupied the space had the same motive, the same goal of turning my heart toward something (or someone) to fill it up with itself. Jesus was talking about me when He said, ". . . the light has come into the world, and people *loved* the darkness rather than the light because their works were evil." Sin had had my attention because it had my heart. In it, I did not merely put up with sin but I loved it. Delighted in it. Adored it. Found ways to deliver to it a bouquet or two of roses so it would know it was on my mind. But this ability to love was not given to me in vain. Lest someone believe that to be sinless one should be loveless. The intention behind my ability to love at all was for it to be lavished on the loveliest One alive and in Him this love was safe. When the Holy Spirit made His home within me, He snatched the blinds down and let the light in. Not only could I see God and His glory with a smile on my face, but I could also see sin for the liar that it was. Light has a way of welcoming in the truth and letting it put its feet up, which in turns means that everything not like it, though it may invite itself over, can't get comfortable enough to stay.

She was nearer to me than before, and I had no idea what I was supposed to do. I was very aware that I wanted to choose God but I didn't know how. And even if I did, would I be *able* to? I'd had plenty of post church revival moments in which I'd try to stop sinning. But after a day or two, I came to find my power to resist sin as feeble as a toddler trying to hold back a hurricane. Before me was the opportunity to do what had always been easy. My mind was more than ready to take hold of her body and wring all of the dignity out of it. My mouth sat anxious waiting for the go-ahead. It knew how to ask others to deny God together, with me. But I stood there, quiet. I didn't know any verses to quote just yet but I figured I should pray. "God, can You help me? Amen."

My current customer was musing over if they wanted extra pickles or extra onions. "Both would be too much," they said to themselves while looking at me. Meanwhile, what had once taken a high priest and a lamb to accomplish was now accessible to me in the middle of a fast-food restaurant. Of course, bystanders wouldn't have noticed the temple, or the veil, or the throne room of God. All they saw was me, a cash register, and an indecisive restaurant patron. But, I was there, face and body bowed before Him. His feet were inches from my hands, I lifted my head just enough to notice mercy and grace coming toward me. Before I knew it, I was back, with the same temptation and with someone else's power.

When salvation has taken place in the life of someone under the sovereign hand of God, they are set free from the penalty of sin *and* its power. In a body without the Spirit, sin is an unshakable king under whose dominion no man can flee. The entire body, with its members, affections, and mind all willfully submit themselves to sin's rule. But when the Spirit of God takes back the body that He created for Himself, He sets it free from the pathetic master that once held it captive and releases it into the marvelous light of its Savior. It is then able to not only want God, but it is actually *able* to obey God. And isn't that what freedom is supposed to be? The ability to not do as I please, but the power to do what is pleasing.

The cash register was open. I stared at the quarters, dimes, pennies, over-used dollar bills and gifts cards that sat inside of it. Whatever would help to distract me from letting lust swallow my mind whole. The pretty girl had ordered on another register and was waiting for her food and I was being sustained by God in her presence. This first trial would be the beginning of many to come, many I would fail, others I would overcome, but I learned something that day. God would be there to help me.

―――――

I missed her eyes the most. To remember them was to remember everything else. When it wasn't her, it was the desire itself that drove me crazy. All I wanted to do was *hold* a woman, just once. I craved the interaction that gave lesbians their names. Titled by an affection that hadn't been lessened by a new birth but instead seemed heightened by it. As if resistance made the thing being resisted a bigger monster than it was before. To my surprise, being a Christian delivered me from the power of sin but in no way did it remove the possibility of temptation.

A common lie thrown far and wide is that if salvation has truly come to someone who is same-sex attracted, then those attractions should immediately vanish. To be cleansed by Jesus, they presume, is to be immune to the enticement of sin. This, we know not to be true because of Jesus. He being completely perfect and yet He still experienced temptation: "For we do not have a high priest who is unable to sympathize with our weaknesses, but one who in every respect has been tempted as we are, yet without sin" (Hebrews 4:15). It should be expected then that any who would follow Him as Lord would still find themselves urged to do what ought not be done. That they would at times, sense in their bodies the temptation to obey *it* and not God. I (and all humans) had the unique disadvantage of having given into the passions of the body so easily and so often before

Christ that after coming under His Lordship, learning how to experience same-sex attraction and not act on it was frustrating. To me, it would've been easier if when God cleansed me of my sin, He also took the taste for it out of my mouth. But even He could understand the grace needed to flee a flavorless feast, at a greater depth than I ever would.

C. S. Lewis wrote:

> A man who gives in to temptation after five minutes simply does not know what it would have been like an hour later. That is why bad people, in one sense, know very little about badness—they have lived a sheltered life by always giving in. We never find out the strength of the evil impulse inside us until we try to fight it: and Christ, because He was the only man who never yielded to temptation, is also the only man who knows to the full what temptation means—the only complete realist.[7]

Among many differences, one between me and Christ, was that with every temptation, He never gave in, once. Sin could never say it made Christ's knees buckle beneath it because an impenetrable holiness kept Him upright at all times. Even in the final hours before His death, when He might've chosen

---

[7] C. S. Lewis, *Mere Christianity* (1952; repr., New York: HarperCollins Publishers, 2015), 142.

another will, or another cup to drink, He, as He'd done always, placed Himself and the wishes of His body under the beautiful will of the Father, showing us all that the body doesn't have to have the final say in our lives.

Still missing her—and any woman for that matter—I felt myself wanting to look toward heaven only to wave goodbye. My back, showing signs of the wear and tear from the cross it was carrying day to day, was weary. The earth started to look like heaven and God, a fading cloud. Standing in the backroom at work, I said to God in my mind, where no one but Him could hear me speak, "God, I am really struggling. I wanna go back so bad. Lord, help me." I stood there straightened up by a familiar interruption. Quieted and listening, my mind held in it this sentence: "Jackie, you have to believe My Word is true, even if it contradicts how you feel."

Temptation was slapping me around like a weightless doll in the hands of an imaginative child. Being tossed between fun and funeral, who would I decide to trust more? What the temptation wanted me to believe or what God had already revealed? The struggle with homosexuality was a battle of faith. To give in to temptation would be to give into unbelief. To decide that the body mattered more than God, or that the pleasure of sin would sustain all that I am better than He. It was incredible how real and tangible and persistent they could be, but their power was an illusion. Jesus had already proven that temptation could be defeated, and He already promised to help me when I came to His throne of grace for it.

It was up to me to believe Him. His Word was authoritative, active, sharp. In it, God spoke and showed us what He is like, how much better He was than anything that had been made, how eligible He was to be our joy, our peace, our portion, how trusting Him, if even a little at a time, would move mountains—the biggest one, being me. These Scriptures were a weapon, a sword, that when used would defeat the flesh. My faith in them would be a shield, that when placed in front of the body would extinguish all satanic attacks coming toward it. Find a human alive and ask them if they have ever lied and you will find none who can say, "No, I have not." But God is not a man, that He would or could lie. Every single thing He has ever or will ever say is true. The simplicity of faith is this: taking God's Word for it. And I might not have felt like it, but I had no choice but to believe Him.

CHAPTER 10

2008

MY CLOTHES WERE BORROWED, again. This time, they were women's clothing. I don't remember if they were skinny jeans or slacks, a form-fitting T-shirt or a size 4 button-up, but I remember them being incredibly uncomfortable.

We walked into the church, not knowing what to expect. It was rather small—more like the size of a large room rather than your typical American sanctuary—which could be a good or bad thing. The Christians I'd met before had a way of looking at me as if I was some kind of ghost. I'd never seen myself as an exotic, untouchable creature, but you'd think that was the case every time I walked into the company of "Christians." They were either oblivious to my existence, or chose to look past me, as if to avoid eye contact and subsequently the obligation to acknowledge me. Or they were of the sort who saw me and stared into me—never speaking, only observing, as a child does a bug. My hope was that these people would be different, different like Jesus.

I had forgotten that women wore clothes that were always five seconds away from being too small for their size. But, I didn't want to deal with the stares and the shame it would carry if I came dressed as myself so I conceded to being someone else, in wardrobe, until service ended at least.

"Good morning!" a woman with a Sunday morning smile said to me as I was on my way to my seat. "What's your name?" she asked, her tone bright and believable. "Jackie," I said. Keeping it short because I was too guarded to say anything more than what was asked of me. I was anxious about this interaction. I didn't know what it would become if it continued. Then she did something I didn't expect.

She looked me in my eyes, unhindered by their cynicism, and nodded her head a bit as she repeated my name. "Jackie," she said again to me, but mainly to herself. It was clear that she wanted to remember it. To not let it pass with the wind but to keep it close at hand. I had never met a stranger who wanted to know my name as if it mattered. My sexuality had been my name for so long that to have someone not treat me according to my assumed sins but according to the identity that my mama gave me felt good. With her, I didn't feel like a project to be fixed but a person to be loved. The two hours that followed were filled with "Hallelujahs," tithe taking, and "Turn your

Bibles to so-and-so." All of which helped me to see another side to this body of people that I never felt safe around but, surprisingly, it wasn't the programs or the preaching that began to lift my distrust of the church. It was the woman who I knew would remember my name if I ever decided to come back.

The gay community is called that for a reason. It *is* a community. A collective of people with different names, social statuses, eating habits, upbringings and more but with one commonality shared among them that made them all more alike than not: their sexuality. What was treated with contempt in the world around them was the secret handshake, the inside joke, the side-eyed smirk that confused most but united them.

The ones who spent their days in a closet came out to play when surrounded by the safety of non-judgmental eyes. The free ones, who had been fearless enough to tell the folks that they shared last names with about them loving differently than expected, were usually the life of the party. After the party, we all knew it meant we were walking back into the land of heterosexuality, where either the closet would shelter us from the burden of honesty, or we'd need to find some measure of courage to simply be who we knew ourselves to be. Stud, Fem, Trade, Bi might've been the different distinctive identities that set us apart from one another. Yet, they all carried a single thread that made us all one. We were gay, together.

So, to leave that community for another one was terrifying, especially when the transition was being made into a community that seemed to be everything but safe. But the group of Christians I began to know and enjoy were ones that did more for me than the gay community could've ever done. They showed me God. The community I called home for a season of my life were all full of laughter and what I'd labeled "life." But the reality was that my gay community was indeed lifeless. They were what I had been, dead. They were still imagebearers, still friends, they still mattered. I still loved them, but I loved God more. They could not help me love who they did not know themselves. The difference between the gay community and the Christian community was not skill, intellect, comfort, humor, or beauty; it was that in one and not the other, God dwelled.

For through Him we both have access by one Spirit to the Father. So then you are no longer foreigners and strangers, but fellow citizens with the saints and members of God's household, built on the foundation of the apostles and prophets, with Christ Jesus Himself as the cornerstone. The whole building, being put together by Him, grows into a holy sanctuary in the Lord. You also are being built together for God's dwelling in the Spirit (Ephesians 2:22).

A community of people who know God cannot be considered regular. What I had once thought to be a collective of mundane and ordinary Christians had now become to me the miraculous in bodily form. Every conversation could, at any moment, be a prayer answered or a burning bush over dinner. They had been made alive by the same God I'd met weeks prior, and they taught me Him better than I would've known Him in solitude. God had put us together and in doing so He had provided the means by which I could learn how to unclothe all that my prior community told me to wear proudly.

———

I met Santoria online. Or should I say, I met her words first. One night when YouTube kept me up past my bedtime, I stumbled onto a video with a woman, name unknown, with Scriptures flying from her mouth like a flock of scattering birds—wing after wing cutting both the sky and the heart of the man to whom she spoke in half.

She was witnessing to a man about Jesus. He was trying, with all of his might, strengthened by an educated form of doubt, to take flight. This interaction was interesting to say the least. Me, being brand-new to the Christian faith, had no name for what this was. What I did know is that I hoped that one day my heart would have enough room to fit as much Bible in it as hers.

Poetry would bring me to LA, where she lived. Before talking for hours in her home, I did poetry at an event thrown by the church where Santoria served as the director of Women's Ministry. I'd emailed them my testimony after learning more about the ministry via YouTube (after Santoria's witnessing video sent me on a binge of all of their other videos). They eventually found out that I was a poet and invited me to join them at their next poetry event. Prior to salvation, I never considered the art of poetry as something worth my participation. Incense-buying, Neo Soul-loving, bongo-playing, brown-skinned and deep-thinking persons fit that mold better than I, until the random, unsolicited urge to write took ahold of me and refused to let go.

Walking into her apartment, I noticed the silence first. After being invited to perform at her church, the pastor made provisions for me to stay in her home. Singleness kept it quiet until ministry brought the noise in. We sat down at her kitchen table, it being fairly clean except for a small stack of mail inches away from her calm hands. She lifted them briefly, only to adjust her hair. One of her locks was being a bit rebellious. Blackened and long enough to touch the table at times, she made sure to put it in its place.

Not many months passed before local churches around St. Louis began to invite me to share what I had written in their conferences and church services. Words were a ministry to me. If God used them to make man and worlds and moons and miracles, then I figured that I'd do well to make sure that after creating my own living thing that God could actually step back and call it good. Good as in glorifying to Him and beneficial for all that He created. But as is expected when humans get their hands on anything, they start thanking themselves for what was made as if their mind was not a borrowed thing.

Santoria, a wise woman used to discerning in people what they couldn't see in themselves, saw it in me. In the same way, she dissected the arrogance of the man she witnessed to on YouTube, she took notice of the same in me. The untangled pride I mistook for confidence as it moved in and out of every long-winded sentence about myself, my life, my thoughts, my wisdom, my gifts, my amateur knowledge of Scripture, and whatever else would help to build the throne on which I could sit. She listened, patiently. The flying birds that flung themselves wildly at the man in the video were tame this time around. I was in his place. Different environment but still under her light, yet it was now not her knowledge of Scripture that intrigued me, but her silent confidence in them.

She had nothing to prove. I had too much to say.

Discipleship was not a word native to the church I joined after coming to the faith. In the church where they remembered my first name, there I learned of the Holy Spirit's power to enter into broken bodies and heal them from the inside out. How He gave out good gifts that, when discovered and displayed, would make Sunday something special. From the pulpit, my once drug-addicted, now delivered, pastor let God tell him what to say; with our Bibles opened wide we prayed loud enough for the walls to know that they were holding in citizens of heaven.

But if asked how the gospel not only changed my life but what its implications were for my day-to-day, I would've had nothing to say. If a follow-up question was posed, such as how the Holy Spirit had not only empowered me to walk in the gifts of the Spirit, but in holiness through the Spirit, I would've called this line of questioning revelatory to say the least. In my short time in Santoria's home, I came to see that her life was full of power in ways that I never knew possible. How when unbelief came near, she faithfully turned Scripture loose to capture and strangle it into submission to a higher will than her own. A gifted woman she was but ungodly she was not. I had known many a person with glorious gifts and satanic lives, but this woman showed me that knowing God was more than knowing about Him and doing things for Him but knowing *Him*.

I moved into Santoria's home a year after God entered my own. Real growth was too hard to find in the church that welcomed me as a new believer. So, through God's guidance and wise counsel I made the move to LA, to be discipled by Santoria, and join the church that introduced us. Her home made for a terrible hiding place. Two decent-sized bedrooms sat adjacent to each other near the rear end of the complex. Two to five steps out of either of the bedrooms, depending on the length of your stride, was the walking distance to the one bathroom being shared by three women: Santoria, her roommate, and me. The crowdedness of her apartment was not what kept privacy and me from becoming acquainted, however. It was that Santoria knew that for her to help me, she had to know me. Friends had known me. My likes, my dislikes. My affinity for Almond Joys and inside-out socks. They'd even known the unspeakable pains that came out of me at times, without words, only tears quickly wiped away by the fear of being labeled weak. For her though, the knowledge she was after was the kind that would seek to know what little and large sins I was withholding from the light. I couldn't kill what I didn't confess or in such an infantile stage of faith as I was, I wouldn't put to death what I believed was keeping me alive. And as for her and her home, she was going to make sure that whoever lived there would actually *do* exactly that. Live.

One morning, I got up a little before 10 a.m. There was a tire shop nearby, blasting mariachi music that bounced and shot sound off of the walls of the apartment complexes that formed an amphitheater around it. The sun was being lazy, refusing to let us all see what outfit he decided to put on before noon. But I knew whenever he got over himself, he'd show off in his own Californian way. Santoria didn't have cable, so most mornings I'd distract myself with social media. Before I sat down at the computer, I noticed a large blue book with a Post-it Note laid on the front cover, positioned, purposely, to the left of the keyboard.

It said, "Before you get on the computer, I want you to read and do Lesson 2 in this book. We will discuss it later when I get home. —San"

After getting over the pre-meditated audacity of Santoria to know exactly what I'd do once awake, and then to interrupt it with something fruitful, I picked up the book to see what she thought would be worth my morning. It was titled, "Seeking Him." I started flipping through the pages, irritably and rushed so I could get it all over with before she came home, landing on a lesson titled "Humility: Coming to God on His Terms."

Soooo, what does this have to do with me? I thought loudly to myself. Irked and unable to gather the boldness to tell Santoria that doing this exercise would just be a game of "Stupid things to do in the morning."

I sat down on the couch behind me and started to read.

What I read had knives in it. Sharp, stainless steel ones, stopping only when a period or paragraph break made them sit still. Some words were shards of a mirror. Each cut showed me what my heart had tried to keep from God. Each sentence told me that pride was not exclusive to the outwardly arrogant people I'd come across, but it also sat inside of all of us. Manifesting in several ways only to be discovered when the Sword of the Spirit pierced through the bone and marrow that housed it.

"Jackie, homosexuality is not your only issue," Santoria told me while discussing my recent diagnoses with pride. "You will have to learn how to die to so much more than that. Whether it's homosexuality, pride, fear, anger, laziness, et cetera, there is more than one sin in you that needs to be overcome, not just your sexuality."

It can be a habit of some to not only have a compartmentalized view of themselves in light of the gospel but to also have a compartmentalized concept of discipleship. Where the entire goal of discipleship in our church communities starts to only be about teaching men and women how to walk free from the loud shouts of their broken sexuality but forgets to teach them how to quiet all of the other noise that the flesh makes. Christ did not die to redeem us in part. Neither did He rise so that we might have life in portions. But with us having a body made for Him, as well as the mind, will, personality, and emotions that it contains, we must understand that God is after us becoming victorious over any and all sin that would hinder the whole person from serving God fully and freely.

Almost daily, I was assigned something to read and/or listen to that helped to give me a clearer understanding of God. Day after day, I was learning how to pray and how to steward money, how to read Scripture rightly, and how to restrain the tongue from the wrong kind of speech, why mercy mattered and how I was to let it lead me.

One night, after watching a movie remake of the story of David and Goliath, I told Santoria how I was struggling with lust. How it was a giant in its own right, intimidating me into listening to its voice, this sin was a talkative one. Never pausing to catch a breath or one to relent from telling me who I should be and what I should do, she said,

"You fight lust with the gospel, Jackie."

"The gospel? How?" I said, unsure whether her advice had any practicality to it. I was hoping she'd provide me with a special sin rebuking prayer, not a petition to just remember the gospel.

"When Jesus died and rose, He gave you power to defeat sin. Literally. Like you don't have to give in. Every single time you are tempted to sin, just remember the reality that Jesus defeated it already. You're not a slave. You are free. You just have to believe that and walk in it."

Bewildered and intrigued as ever, I looked up at her and said, "So you're telling me that the gospel is all I need to fight sin?"

Trying to contain the small giggle welling up in her chest from the sincerity of my question, Santoria, full of confidence, responded while looking toward my direction, "Yes, Jackie. The gospel didn't just save you, it also keeps you."

———

In an effort to be kept by some other means, many saints have found themselves on a path paved by self-righteousness and good works and not the gospel. The gospel being that a Holy God created a people for Himself, they all sinned, breaking His divine laws. In doing so, they all deserved the judgment that a righteous God is required to pronounce, but God's love moved Him to send His Son Jesus, God in the flesh, to carry the sins of many, be judged as they should've been so that they can live the life that they could never merit. Jesus, then, having all power to do this and more, rose from the dead, defeating death, and commanded all to repent and believe in His name; and that for those that do by grace, they will be saved and filled with the Holy Spirit, Who, in turn, has sealed them for the day of redemption when all of the saints will continue in the eternal life they received the day that they believed.

Some would have us to believe that it is possible to graduate from Christ's gospel. To treat it as if it was no different than Similac or high chairs, or learning how to tie your shoes only so you can move on to doing better things with your feet.

But reality would have it that a departure from dependence on the gospel would be a departure from dependence on Christ Himself.

"Therefore, as you have received Christ Jesus the Lord, so walk in him, rooted and built up in him and established in the faith, just as you were taught, abounding in thanksgiving" (Colossians 2:6–7).

I received Christ by faith in His gospel. And it was in and through His gospel that I saw God. In my seeing God, through the eyes of faith, illuminated and bright with the gospel's light, sin could not compare to the King of Glory. I'd laid eyes on Someone worth dying for because His death had both lifted my own and ensured that I would be able to die to all that kept me from Life.

As Jeff Vanderstelt stated so well, "The gospel doesn't just bring about forgiveness of sins and save us from hell. The gospel of Jesus Christ empowers us to live a whole new life today by the same Spirit who raised Jesus from the dead."[8]

How is it then that I would think that God would provide another way for me to walk freely that did not find its pulse in His gospel? I was not to assume that the gospel was only an introduction to Jesus. I needed to cling to, meditate on,

---

[8] Jeff Vanderstelt, *Gospel Fluency* (Wheaton, IL: Crossway, 2017), 73.

trust in, believe always, this gospel daily, with the same kind of unhindered desperation that led me to it the first time. In being anchored in this gospel, I would be holding onto God.

John Piper writes:

> The ultimate aim of the gospel is the display of God's glory and the removal of every obstacle to our seeing it and savoring it as our highest treasure. "Behold your God!" is the most gracious command and best gift of the gospel. If we do not see him and savor him as our greatest fortune, we have not obeyed or believed the gospel.[9]

A consistent look into the Scriptures would remind me of the gospel—from Genesis, from the Old Testament narratives of sacrifices and temples and prophets and priests all pointing forward to the New Testament and Jesus, unto Revelation, with the consummation of Jesus' final victory, with all of His own, praising Him as a slain Lamb even as He stands as a conquering King. Even now, His bride, the local church, is the constant reminder of His death, burial, and resurrection. As they sing of His victory, pray at His feet, preach about His beauty, break the bread and drink the wine, remembering how both His body and blood has made us all free.

---

[9] John Piper, *God Is the Gospel* (Wheaton, IL: Crossway, 2005), 56.

The gospel of God saved my life, in others He'd done the same. And in doing so, my life when around theirs, could look more like His. Who was I to think I could look like the triune God by trying to *live* alone.

CHAPTER 11

2008–2014

I DON'T KNOW HOW it feels to be a woman anymore." I had spent time in the mirror and noticed the girlishness was gone. My eyelashes were still long enough to hide under. But they could not keep the hardness in my eyes from scaring away the pretty that used to peek through. Heck, it even scared me. Who was this person looking back at me? They looked familiar. I knew I'd seen that nose before. And those eyes, those "Don't hurt me or I'll break inside of myself again" eyes. I'd seen them on my mama and daddy's face, but this person couldn't possibly have their blood. They had a daughter. But what stood, staring at me, wasn't the girl I'd seen in family pictures. Or *was she*, still?

A year before I moved to LA, and one day after the Holy Spirit moved inside of me, I was doing the painful work of breaking up with my girlfriend. Her tears were too loud to listen to without regret. I heard her wipe her face. After breathing out the pain, the confusion of it all parted her mouth to ask me, "Why? Why are you doing this?" It made sense for her to ask it. She knew how much I loved her, how childish my face got when she was around, with a different kind of blushing that only colored the way my eyes spread out while leaving my cheeks unblemished. She'd never seen it in person, but she knew my heart by name.

To leave her, us, our love, made no sense apart from the divine doing of God. She was both my woman and my idol. An unqualified god without an ounce of deity. She was the eye Jesus said to gouge out and the right hand He commanded me to cut off (Matthew 5:29–30). Though it was as painful as the extreme act of removing a part of the body, it was better for me to lose her than to lose my soul.

"I just . . . gotta live for God now," I said with a tear-broken voice, ending us and what felt like my own undoing. A new identity was to come after I hung up. I thought about the mirror and how I'd forgotten what I looked like. How the person I saw in front of me did not look like my mama or the daughter she raised. In seeing God the night before, I also wanted to see where the girl in me had gone and if she could ever come back. Being a woman was something I no longer knew how to be, but the real question was, had I ever known?

———

A week had passed since becoming new, but outwardly not many knew the difference. I didn't own anything you'd buy in women's sections nor did I really want to. But I wore what I had until I could afford to buy what would honor what I was. Starting small, I bought a real bra. One that would affirm the way God had made my chest instead of concealment. Boxers were, though comfortable, utterly useless for me. I began to lay them aside every morning to step foot inside of women's underwear instead, which unexpectedly adjusted the way my legs made my entire body move. The harsh way in which I stepped into the day started to smoothen itself out, like a finger-painted song. The act of doing something so secret and small, such as wearing what other women wore under their clothing began to draw that forgotten girl out of me. It was a daily ritual of repentance—the first domino in a long line for the rest of my day. Nobody knew but me. But everybody could tell something was different, even if they didn't know what.

I stood outside of Forever 21, irked as ever. The little adjustments made in secret were not to be compared to what came next. In this store, on the hangers, folded on shelves, tried on, bought and returned was more than fabric shaped into shirts; it was a new identity—a new way of introducing myself to the world. Girl after girl entered in, smiling wide, ready to spend and carry their femininity in bright yellow bags. There was a normalcy to their delight. Purchasing a floral sundress or a pair of ripped skinny jeans that helped their hips shine was not a monumental achievement, or even a terrifying act of reclaiming their womanhood; it was all they knew how to be—girls, who loved being just that and I could not relate.

The entire scene made me want to run somewhere else, with clothes that I could hide behind and never be found, where the insecure girl, unsure of her body and why God gave it to her could be left to her own confusion instead of being positioned to deal with them. But, I figured, I had done much harder things than this. If I could leave the love of my life for the Lover of my soul, then changing my clothes, though difficult, would not be as horrific as it seemed.

Inside of my own bright yellow bag was a blue long-sleeved shirt, with marble-colored buttons and red roses on each side. Next to it, were two pairs of skinny jeans, a gray, yet thin knit sweater and a maroon vest lined with white wool. I had my *own* clothes to wear now. Ones that, when worn, would be its own kind of baptism. While immersing myself in something as natural as women's clothing would not cleanse me of my masculine ways, just as water could not wash away my sins, it would be a declaration. A symbolic shout that the woman that once was lost had now been found. She had been reclaimed and unburied. Her being brought back to life was not meant to be hidden by clothing that told the world a different creation story. One that made her bodily distinctions unimportant. Disrobing myself of clothing that projected an image unlike the one I was born as was not me trying to save myself but rather, it was an act of reminding myself of who I was made to be.

Womanhood is a strange thing, to me at least. Possibly, because the way it was defined, then given to me, was not at all what it began as or was intended to be. By the time I was a girl old enough to listen, *it* had been packaged differently. Like a game of telephone, the message first whispered by God was misunderstood, intentionally and accidentally edited and then sent to me as a formula for being a woman in the world. By the time I'd received it though, I knew it couldn't have possibly been meant for *me*. I was too aggressive for the kind of low-to-the-ground women they told me God loved. My edges were too rough to measure up to the soft ones men wanted to marry and deliver their offspring. Those women didn't look like me. I couldn't find one feature, either in their light cloudless voices or in the dainty, gravity-less ways in which they entered rooms, that imaged who I knew myself to be. I was too hard, too mean, too declarative, too sure of my words, too heavy to subdue, too unlike pink, too much like gray, too normal to notice, and too much like myself to be woman enough for everybody else.

It is not a shock, then, that I had no clue of who I was, seeing that, unbeknownst to me, I'd spent my life staring at

a stereotype instead of God. He, not the sloppily drawn cari-
catures being tossed around by culture, would be honest and
accurate when telling me about womanhood because He made
it and me.

Elisabeth Elliott wrote:

> To understand the meaning of womanhood we
> have to start with God. If He is indeed "Creator of
> all things visible and invisible" He is certainly in
> charge of all things, visible and invisible, stupen-
> dous and minuscule, magnificent and trivial. God
> has to be in charge of details if He is going to be
> in charge of the overall design.[10]

Being a woman was not something I needed to learn, per
se. Woman is what I already was. It is unhelpful to paint a picture of womanhood that only involves behavior and not how
this behavior involves the body. Eve was called woman before
she ever behaved like one. Though I was a woman biologically,
I needed to learn how to be one in the fullest since by mirror-
ing Christ both in body and behavior. As I got to know God
better, He surely showed me how.

---

[10] Elisabeth Elliott, *Let Me Be a Woman* (1976; Carol Stream, IL:
Tyndale, 1999), 8.

———

I remember seeing the time He walked inside the temple. In one area were tables. Behind them were men with quick hands and wide eyes. People, some clearly not native to the soil they stood on, held out their hands, peeled back their fingers to reveal the coins of their country. The businessmen, with urgent and quick movements as if to sift out the temple traffic to make room for more, placed another currency in their customers' hands. These local coins would allow them to purchase what had brought them to the temple in the first place: a sacrifice. They didn't have to travel far from the money changers to get a sacrifice however; they only needed to walk toward the sound of frustrated wings flapping against caged metal.

They'd come to worship and needed something unblemished, unlike themselves, to put before God. They were hoping that the slaughter of a white dove would be music to His ears instead of the noisiness of their sins but when God arrived, the sight before Him looked nothing like a hallelujah. It didn't even sound like heaven. Jesus, full of the Holy Spirit, walked toward the table where the money changers were doing business as usual. His hands, the same hands that just unveiled two sets of blind eyes, swift and passionate in their touch, lifted the table from its place. The coins it held flew up and glittered like several sparkling countries. Those selling the doves found themselves misplaced from their chairs as they saw their seats take flight. Jesus, controlled and fueled by everything reverent reminded all who had an ear to hear of who the temple belonged to and what belonged in it. It was God's and in it belonged prayer.

From a distance, Jesus could've been accused of many things. One being, having flipped over tables and chairs in the temple, especially in front of company, was not the "gentle Jesus, meek and mild" description we may have learned about in Sunday school. But to say so would be tiptoeing toward blasphemy. As if, at any time, in heaven and on the earth, Jesus stopped bearing the Spirit's fruit—Jesus was at all times fully, even in the zealous way with which He flipped the temple back on its knees, walking in meekness.

For a woman such as myself, this sight of Jesus dismantled the notion that to be meek, as commanded by God through Peter, meant that I was to be relegated to the position of a doormat. Or better yet, a woman who treated her voice like it was secret. The way Jesus was driven by His commitment to His Father and the truth. In the same way, to have a quiet and gentle spirit—a call given to women—would not mean I had to abandon all that I am, limp along in life, silence my personality in the name of obedience, but instead it meant that I could authentically be the woman God made me as, while anchored in the truth and controlled by the Spirit. When led by Him, when wanting to place my rights above His honor, humility would place its hand over my heart, keeping it still and settled with peace until what was worth being said or done happened in love. Out of a deep wanting for what belonged to God to be recognized and respected.

Figuring out what it meant to be a meek woman helped me begin unraveling all the other misconceptions of womanhood told to me by bad listeners. By looking to God's Word for how to be a woman, I found what God intended when He gave me this call. God's image is what womanhood was born out of. Not the 1950s Polaroids of white women baking cookies while talking loud enough to be heard and quiet enough to not call attention to their intellect. Neither that nor the pictures of women, jaded and committed to speaking *at* men like they were negligent children or wayward dogs you don't trust without a leash. The self-proclaimed "liberated woman" was far beyond the picture God cared for me to become. The temple being used rightly was important to Jesus, and I felt as if there was a shared passion for my womanhood. How I moved about the world as a woman mattered to God. It started to matter to me, more than ever, when I found out I was pregnant with a girl.

———

I got pregnant on my honeymoon.

Five weeks after becoming one flesh with the only man I'd ever *known*, a test with two symmetrical lines split my world in half. I was already a new wife with a new last name, unusually confident that my past wouldn't have the final say on my future. I didn't expect a baby to find their way included in it so soon though. I figured it would've been better for them and me if they chose to arrive after I'd learned how to hug more often and cry less silently. The night after the doctor told us that my body was carrying a girl, I cried.

I'm having a girl?! I thought. I barely know how to be one myself. My husband, laid next to me, sleeping as if the world never moved as he dreamt, but I stared toward the ceiling afraid of tomorrow. I knew that my own version of womanhood would be the model in which my daughter would squeeze her own personal womanhood into. My words wouldn't matter as much as my life would.

In my living, loving, speaking, silence, submission, moving modestly, modeling the goodness of God in my gender, my daughter would learn from me first. That night, newly married and soon to be mothering a girl made in God's image, I decided that if I could teach my daughter anything about herself, it would be that because a good God made the woman, then *being* a woman was a *good* thing.

The next day, I started living like it.

CHAPTER 12

2009–2014

HE WAS ATTRACTIVE BUT I wasn't attracted. I could see why women had been a thorn for him. I'd been a Christian for less than a year and men didn't catch my eye in the least. If it were up to me, at least at that point, I would've wanted to take hold of that weird thing in women that made them gasp when they saw a man that snatched the breath out of their day. How they'd find a friend and tell her to look at his face. Then ask her, "Isn't he so cute?" And wait for her answer in the form of a smile that said nothing and, "Yes, girl!" at the same time. These communal moments of attraction shared between friends would hopefully involve me one day, but until then I only wanted to get to know this poet from Chicago because his story reminded me of my own.

No one was quiet. Fingers snapped. Hands patterned themselves after drums and filled the room with music. There wasn't a tambourine in sight, but no one would've noticed the difference. As arms, affirmative and wild, waved toward the ceiling, everyone felt the life they were trying to give. Sometimes there was laughter. Other times tears. Here, humanity had a place to go. Here, truth was proud of itself. Here, you could tell it had no shame. It told us all who it was and why it belonged and we loved it.

The stage was the center of attention. One mic, and usually one poet, stood behind it. These artists were magical in how they could turn sentences into scenes that sometimes flew above our heads and gave us glimpses into another world. Next up to the mic were two poets from Chicago, another world to most, including me. I'd heard the stories of it having more bullet holes than homes, and how the police protected nobody but their own. Somewhere, somehow, they had forgotten to mention beauty, and how she lived in Chi-town too. She was the reason Martin, Ali, Barack, and Michelle all called her home at one time or another. Even God was there. Of course, He didn't have an address; He didn't even have a place to lay His head that time in Jerusalem, but that didn't keep Him from dwelling in the big city on the Lake. He'd called out hundreds, maybe thousands of people in between Lake Michigan and the city limits and turned them into a house holy enough for Him to live in. Out of these Christians came the two poets that walked onto the stage in LA.

I'd come to perform but I had to wait until the rest of the lineup had finished. While the crowd clapped loud enough to make the poets feel welcomed, I noticed one of them. He stepped toward the mic, hesitantly. Not timid, but I could tell he was unsure if what would come out would match the color of his skin. It looked like coffee with caffeine in it—the strong kind that will wake a room up. He started to speak and his voice caught me off guard. I didn't expect it to sound so heavy.

I couldn't help but pay attention to everything he said. He was doing a poem about his past—a past full of women he'd never married, some he barely loved, but all he laid bare with. His forgiven sins were put before us, and it was clear that He was proud of the grace of God. He talked about his promiscuity in past tense. He hadn't forgotten one bit of what he'd done, but he wanted us to know that God remembered mercy when He thought of him.

———

Preston became my friend after he messaged me on Facebook asking my advice on a poem he was writing. I lived in LA. He was in Chicago. But we talked like our cities were three blocks away. Almost weekly, we'd sit up talking about everything under the sun. From how my daddy left me hanging more than strange fruit to how his mama thought the street would eventually eat him alive. He told me silly things too, like how his fourth-grade teacher refused to let him use the restroom and dared him to use it another way if he kept talking back. She didn't know, or probably didn't care, that she had a fearless boy in her classroom. He'd seen too much in his life to be afraid of suspension so he pulled his pants down and relieved himself in front of the classroom, inside of the trash can, underneath the pencil sharpener. And he hadn't changed much since. Maturity constrained the rebellion in his bones, but boldness didn't plan on leaving anytime soon. I heard it in every story we shared. It sat perched on his tongue and flew out and into everything everybody else was afraid of, including me.

"The guys are afraid of you."

"Why though?" I looked at him, with no regard for how much my tone sounded like an accusation instead of a question. Preston was tapping the screen of his phone and simultaneously moving his pointer finger up and down it, looking for anything to keep his ADD at bay. "I don't know. They just said you were intimidating. Like, they think you pretty but they scared to approach you."

I'd been told plenty of times, by more people than I preferred, that my face looked more solemn than safe. They'd comment on my eyes and how they said more than my mouth did. They thought they'd heard them telling whoever looked at them, "Get away," or, "Who told you to come near?" And they were.

But they were more long-winded than anybody gave them credit for, probably because no one asked my eyes how they'd gotten that way. If someone did, they would've told them about the time they looked at my daddy as he told me, with the calmest voice I'd ever heard, that if I never talked to him again he wouldn't care. Or the time I watched my entire third-grade classroom become a lynch mob of eight-year-old bullies, against me, my hair, my gap, my skin, my face, my crying face, my hiding-in-my-arms face, my "Why won't they leave me alone, don't they see that they've broken me already" face. My eyes knew why I kept them from smiling more. I was too afraid of what people would do when they found out I could break. Looking up from the distraction in his hands, Preston looked at me, sitting on a bright red couch to his right and said nonchalantly, "That's lame though, cuz I ain't afraid of you. I think you cool."

Preston didn't know that that's what made him different. Distinct. Set apart. He saw me like God did, a woman with more baggage than she had the strength to carry, but still going somewhere. And he wasn't afraid to be my friend on the way. His sense of manhood wasn't thrown into frenzy when it came in contact with my complex femininity.

It was hard not to notice that Preston was different, and notice myself hoping the best about men in general. This didn't suit me too well after a lifetime of believing men were all no different than the boy who abused me and the father that

121

failed me, but Preston showed me another side. There were times when Preston's compassion shocked me. He had an *actual* concern for more people than himself. Who would've known that it was possible for a man to *love*, for him to have a heart that let other people come inside, a mind that chose to care about other things that mattered to other people? He remembered birthdays, and middle names, and last week's prayer requests, asked you how you were doing on Monday morning, as if he'd just finished talking to God about you before work. Shoot, I thought Jesus was the only man who practiced what He preached, but Preston was a sermon without words. His character started slowly disintegrating the bricks pain had set up that worked to keep the fear in and the beauty out. As it did, my heart breathed deep and let out an affection with his name on it. And, I had no idea what to do with it.

———

"Santoria, I think I might like Preston." It even sounded strange saying it out loud. Like being the first one to say, "I love you." I told her not mainly because I wanted advice, but because I wanted her to tell me to put it to death. This attraction, in my opinion, could've been coming from an unholy place. Or maybe even something less urgent than morality—maybe I was just bored.

I'd been a Christian for almost three years now, and I might've missed how it felt to have a crush, to have someone to text at all hours of the day, talking about nothing and everything, while your friends notice you smiling at your phone and ask you his name. Maybe my heart just wanted *that*, not him. If it did, I could easily turn my attention elsewhere, onto something less terrifying, but just as distracting—like books, or poetry, or something without a pulse. But if it *was* a real desire for *him* and not the idea of him, I, not *it*, would have to die to the fear that had been alive in me for as long as I could remember.

"Tell God about it," Santoria said. It would've been unusual if she didn't bring God into it somehow. "If it's another motive, God will show you. If it's a real attraction, God will help you." And that's what I did.

A year went by without me saying one word to Preston about how I felt and many words to God. During the silence, we saw each other frequently, mainly at poetry events in Chicago or LA. Before and after we'd still laugh the moon to sleep, and quickly change the subject into a debate on theology, that eventually turned into us swapping childhood stories. Those stories turned into a discussion on dreams not yet realized.

With the amount of time that passed and the steady stream of prayers sent heavenward, I figured that the developing affection I'd felt a year prior would excuse itself. But it chose to grow. Not like weeds. Weeds are an ugly, unworthy description of what my heart was doing to me. This growth was what Nikki Giovani described once when she wrote about the rose and how it grew from concrete. Concrete could've been what my heart was made of if God didn't replace it with flesh. What came out of it wasn't expected by the street itself, or the world it sat in, but it grew anyway. It didn't need permission, only grace. Only God could do something so strange. Like make something beautiful rise out of the ground. He did it before with His body, and now in mine, like a rose out of concrete, grew my love for a man.

And not *any* man or every man but a man named Preston. At first, this budding attraction was more about *him* than it was about his gender. My affection for the person he was eventually produced in me a desire for *all* that he was—his personality and his manliness. A weird sight and one difficult to understand when you're used to seeing flowers come out of better places, but it was a beautiful one all the same.

I always wondered if anyone could tell that I talked to God about Preston. I tried my best to keep the things I told God from showing in my body. I'd seen how friends let their teeth tell on them. One smile in the direction of the man they wanted to love them back gave all of their secrets away. Mine were becoming hard to hide when he came around though. I was being tempted to stare too long, keep my hands near his, ask for hugs way before it was time to go and hours after we'd already said, "Goodbye." The poker face was smirking too much to do its job, so I went home one night and told God about it.

Seated on my bed, positioned the same way I would if I were about to play one round of cards, "God, I don't know what Your will is for me and Preston, but if it's Your will for us to be together, then place it on his heart to pursue me. But if it's not Your will, then please give me the self-control to treat him like a brother in Christ and not a crush." God heard it and had already been answering weeks before I'd asked. He'd already been interrupting Preston's prayers by putting me in them. Showing him me as he prayed for a wife. Telling him about us as being more than what we'd thought we were and how the next step would be for him to call a spade a spade by telling me the truth. And he did.

I'd never heard so much insecurity in his voice. It reminded me of someone crossing a busy street. How their face is set on moving forward but their legs feel the cars coming and know that the only thing keeping them from a crash is if they keep going. Preston was walking into unknown territory. He had no idea that I liked looking at him or that I wanted to feel his hands, and hug him whenever I felt like it. All he knew was that I was the only woman that kept his attention. The way I walked into rooms didn't scare him. All he knew was that he liked my face and my mind. How he enjoyed listening to me talk and how he trusted what I said. He knew I would be honest. He knew a lying woman wasn't worth his heart. Many had seen his body but that heart had been kept from seeing the light of day, but when God told him "Go" he did.

———

Moving forward was a battle if I'd ever known one. I wasn't alive through any wars. Hadn't had the chance to hear from anybody's granddaddy about what he'd seen. And how it woke him up at night. How thunder made him feel like the enemy discovered where he'd been hiding and how the rain tapping on the window sounded like bullets. How, when his oldest was a baby, he got certain sounds all mixed up in his head. At times, it was hard to decipher if what he heard in the other room were her cries or if another soldier in his platoon had lost his leg. How sometimes, if he closed his eyes too long, the darkness made him see things. Bad things. Things that reminded him of being barely out of high school and having to walk over a fresh body. How all he wanted to do was call his mama and hear her voice, but his country had better things for him to do with his youth. The question is, how's a man supposed to act normal when he's seen death more than sleep? Why would we expect him not be afraid of the dark, to go on with life as usual as if there wasn't always something to remind him of war?

I was excited that God answered my prayer, and that both my and Preston's feelings for each other were out on the table, but it triggered something in me I didn't expect. When he was only my friend, I could be known on my own terms. From a distance, sure, he could know my daddy's name, what I liked to eat on weekdays, and even learn about why I cried so quietly. But this *new,* more intentional relationship we were stepping into scared me. Even my mind couldn't handle it. It made me look at Preston differently. I got suspicious. He wasn't my friend anymore. He was a threat. Because he was a man. And men hurt things, people, me. They always did. They always hurt what they touched. Like they came into this world only to feed off the bones of women. Maybe they were trying to get back at God for taking their ribs apart to make her. Maybe they thought that the more they tore her apart, the more likely they could put themselves back together again. I didn't want Preston to have that kind of power. But I felt like he did.

When I said yes to his pursuit, a war started between us. I didn't know how to receive his love, and he didn't know how to give it. The girl he'd met in LA was not the same one he spoke with over dinner. She'd shut down, gone somewhere only consistency would bring back. It was all so uncomfortable, like learning a language you were always too afraid to speak. Those hugs I thought I wanted made me cringe. Having to readjust the way my arms embraced his body, because he was not a woman whose waist I could place my hands around and pull close, annoyed me. He was a grown man with a solid back with shoulders that read, "Put your arms here instead." His hands were larger than mine. They'd find their way to the small cleft in my back and sit there, gently. Like they knew my body was supposed to be held. It didn't feel endearing or sweet; it felt like a taunt, like they were trying to remind me that he was stronger. He'd place his head near the blade of my shoulder, like a child looking for the warm corners of their mother's body to rest on, and all I could feel was his facial hair graze my chin. I'd feel the violent urge to get it away from me. I'd remember how different it felt to hug a woman, whose hands felt careless and unassuming, and whose face didn't bear the fruit of testosterone. Oh, how I wanted it all to end. For the entire experience to not be so complicated and an adventure I didn't know I signed up for.

———

We flew to Trinidad together to do a poetry event we were both booked for. Five months had passed since we'd started dating and nothing had gotten easier. We were being counseled by a few leaders from my church, and I was getting my own separate counseling to help me find grace in the chaos. I'd moved to Chicago to work for a Christian non-profit and was getting used to the frequency of seeing Preston's face and dealing with the arguments that followed it. What kept us committed, and unwilling to find a wider road to travel on was we knew, that even in the craziness of our relationship, God wanted us together. In no point of my knowing Him had I ever seen Him call me toward life and it not be paved with tribulation. In this, God was up to something good but, for now, the bad was all around.

When we arrived on the island, I was frustrated. I'd been burdened by a persistent temptation. By day, my memory brought old ghosts around to tell me how good death used to feel. It wasn't an easy thing to not believe that sometimes. To not tell myself that women didn't look better than God, but I knew better than that. By night, my dreams were haunted. What I turned to prayer and Scripture and confession to keep out of my heart came back with a vengeance when the sun went down. I saw my girlfriend every time I went to sleep. I'd hear her voice and miss her. Waking up to fight another day was only half the battle. It was forgetting all that I saw before I did that took just as much courage.

My faith couldn't stand up to that kind of relentless assault. It got weaker by the day from having to deny so much, so often. After my and Preston's poetry event, we sat next to each other watching the NBA finals. He'd noticed the dark cloud I was under and was tired of acting like he didn't see it. And feel it. And smell its fury coming *at* him every time I moved.

"What is wrong with you? Like, why are you acting so dang mean to me?"

He sounded angry. Like all of the months of my warlike behavior had finally gotten to him. I snapped, without raising my voice.

"You know what, I don't even know why I'm with you."

Unbelief had taken my hope and my tongue.

"Like, I just don't understand why I'm not with women. Because I don't want to be with you."

I'd been thinking it all week and couldn't hold the doubt in any more. If God wanted us together, He would have to do it because I couldn't. I wasn't Him. I couldn't make the world and everybody in it, hold up the sun, command the moon, number the stars, humble the proud, exalt the humble, split the Red Sea, heal lepers, or raise the dead. An angel never told my mama she was about to give birth to God. My daddy didn't have all of heaven singing his name. If I'd been God, I could've done the impossible by making a gay-girl-turned-Christian love a man well. But I wasn't, therefore I couldn't, so I gave up.

––––––––

After I got back to Chicago, I knew we were over for good. There was no way a man could resurrect after that. I'd killed us, and I partly felt some relief about it.

My first *real* heterosexual relationship was harder than I'd ever imagined. The freedom, the possibility of being able to not care, and not have to explain why, made me feel good. But the guilt, it was heavier than being free. How could I break the heart of the first man I'd ever *wanted* to love and did love, just not out loud. He'd been nothing but willing—willing to lay down in front of a speeding train or jump in front of the smiling mouth of a gun ready to blow him back out of my life.

My past haunted me and now us. It wouldn't let me, now us, go. It was keeping me, now us, back. And I let it. And in many ways, I couldn't help it. Just like the granddaddy I'd never talked to couldn't help but see war when he closed his eyes, I couldn't help but think about war when I looked into Preston's. But, I'd walked away from those eyes and the peace treaty they so desperately wanted me to make.

It was midday, and I hadn't spoken to Preston yet. My job at the time had a prayer room. There was nothing spiritual about it. Couches and Bibles were the only noticeable decorations. I sat down, with the weight of a wearied soul, heavy now with knowing I'd hurt my friend. Pain being bigger than me can't naturally fit inside my body or stay put for too long before it starts seeping out in various ways. As it made its way up my chest, it sounded like when the wind catches fire. Breathing, I tried to hold it in, but that only made it move quicker.

Before I knew it, pain was on my lap. It had escaped out of my eyes and onto my face. I covered it with my hands, hoping to catch it so that it wouldn't mess anything else up but it kept coming anyway. It got faster and less disciplined each time I thought about God and what I'd done to the son He'd sent to love me. My phone buzzed, which for a second, reminded me of being stung and the delayed pain that comes after it. I wiped the leftover grief off of my hands and picked up my phone to see who cared to contact me. A quick glance at the top of the message spelled Preston's name. I knew below it would only be a reminder of how I'd desecrated our relationship with my fear. Was he messaging me only to torture and tell me how much of a murderer I am? He clearly didn't have much to say. Through the tears, I could see that the message was short. *Brevity is a good thing*, I thought. *The quicker I can read it, the less I have to reply to.* I looked closer, and read the words, "I Love You."

The tears returned, but now, they came from a different place. Pain hadn't gone anywhere, but now confusion and shock took up some of its space. How is it that I'd found a man that had the audacity to love *me*. After I'd told him, "No!" After I'd denied him access to this heart he only wanted to hold? How dare he be unlike my daddy? Who told him he could stay? What promise had he believed that kept him alive and unwilling to let us die? I'm sure it was what the apostle Paul wrote to the Ephesians. What else could it have been? If not Jesus and His love for a stiff-necked people, then who? What other story was as good as that, and as relevant for us, than the news that Jesus laid down His life for a bride that didn't want Him in her own? Preston didn't love me because he was a hopeless romantic. Our situation according to a worldly standard *was* hopeless. But he had another reference point to draw strength from: the gospel. He loved me because he loved God *more*.

———

A month later, Preston walked on stage. The poetry event we'd met at four years earlier had grown from two hundred people in a Los Angeles warehouse to thirty-five hundred people, still loud and in love with poetry, wall to wall inside of a large Californian church. I sat in the front row, waiting on him to "spit."

The room, silent, his eyes nervous, his mouth opened,

"The air was April. We were friends back then, with no worries or expectations between us, just chemistry we only talked about with our body language. Both poets with tongues so sharp you would never guess they were made from the same flesh we daily died to. We always had our way with words, but we never took advantage of them. We respected the art form of poetry God placed in our hearts as if we could literally feel King David's blood galloping through our veins. I would miss those mornings, when we arose from our slumber drained from the previous night when we talked the moon to sleep and the stars grew tired of our company. How we manhandled our moments together, and how our dominant personalities coexisted well, like two humble kings at a feast, respect being the cornerstone of the relationship.

This was us in retrospect. This was us before our true feelings shot from our hearts, flew out of our mouths, and landed in each other's lives like two beautiful missiles we didn't quite know what to do with. Admiring the way they were well-constructed but fearing that they might explode at anytime, to blow off the limbs of our emotions. I knew because our relationship brought out the war in her. Her heart became a battlefield. Her tongue turned into a shield and her eyes were swords that cut deep with every stare. Her warrior-like behavior shook the marrow out of my bones, confused about how I became the enemy in the matter of months. Started to question her love for me. And then one day the Lord spoke and said, 'Preston. If you had been wounded in battle too many times to count, you would have adopted some guerilla war-type tactics too. I'm calling you to love her not like you but like Me.'"[11]

When he was done, he asked me to be his wife. I answered him, willingly. He could have my yes, but it would be harder for him to have my trust.

---

[11] "Journey to Covenant" by Preston Perry.

CHAPTER 13

2013–2014

SO, YOU KNOW YOU gotta start trusting me now."

We'd only been engaged for two minutes. In the time it took to walk from the stage to the green room, Preston took advantage of our first moments alone to tell me what to do. He meant well, of course. To him, he believed he'd proven that his hands could hold my heartbeat and not ruin its rhythm. He'd loved me in ways that shocked even him. This, plus a bent knee, glad smile, and a request to be his until God took me home meant that it was time to "let go" now (or so he thought).

For me, I needed more than time and love and a ring.

I needed God, again.

We started premarital counseling shortly after our engagement with our pastor and his wife. They led us in the typical survey of marriage-related Bible texts in the beginning of our time that would usually end with prayer and an inquiry on the state of our purity. Premarital counseling became one of the few places where our arguments were made public with the hope of a resolution.

Our disagreements weren't creative or new. They were repetitive. He felt like I wasn't respectful enough. I felt that he wasn't patient enough. He wanted me to be more gentle. I wanted him to understand why I wasn't. He wanted me to stop treating him like I was waiting on him to hurt me. I wanted him to realize that I didn't know how.

It was the not knowing *how* to live like I'd never been hurt that frustrated me most. I'd done harder things. I'd told the woman whose love I'd loved most goodbye. I'd said hello to God. I'd changed my clothes. Committed to a local church. Found new friends, new hobbies, new everything. But for some reason, I couldn't make *me* new enough to love Preston fearlessly.

Loving women was an easy thing for me. I didn't have to work to give them me. They could have it all—my unhidden tears, my untold stories, my freest self. Preston loved me like God. But no matter how loving he chose to be, he was still a man. A man that wasn't God. A human man that could forget God if he wanted to. Then love me. Me, a fragile woman. Me, a scared girl. Me, someone that just wanted not to care so much about keeping the pain out that I could never let love come in.

In between the good days—when we remembered how to be friends—and the less-than-good days when we threw our frustrations at each other like whips, I prayed. March 1, the date of our wedding, was approaching and fear was insisting on walking me down the aisle.

I couldn't let fear hold my hand. Even though it was a familiar palm, a consistent one even, I knew it would only work to separate what God was going to join together. I couldn't just let it go without another hand to take its place. I couldn't go down that aisle alone. My legs would most likely stop half way and tell my body to go back—to do what's easy, to live fearing the goodness of God.

So to God, I prayed. I'd been afraid for too long to believe I'd be able to undo it all without His help. And that is most likely what God was wanting the entire time. My trust.

God did not primarily want me to trust in Preston, but in Him. This relationship, this engagement, and this eventual marriage, was being used by God to force me to deal with the portions of my heart I'd never let God touch. Fear had been taking up way too much space, and God had never been one to share the heart of His children with lies. So Preston, unbeknownst to him, was God's refining fire.

If it were all as easy as I'd wanted it to be I would've been happy, but I doubt I would've been whole. God had and was saving all of me. He wanted my mind *and* my emotions. My purity *and* my peace. My body *and* my battles. This Lord I'd now known for six years was loving me by exposing me. An uncomfortable kind of sanctification by way of the only man I was willing to give my "I do" to.

Down the aisle, I walked—still terrified, but this time my relationship with fear was different. This time, the fear had opposition. It would not be able to persist with ease, with its feet kicked up on the couch and a glass of lemonade to welcome it home.

With each step toward the man I knew I loved, faith told my legs what to do. Faith let fear know where it could go: away.

Underneath my gown, white with a train, was a fight none of the guests could see. They saw my smile and my upright neck and didn't know what had made me so confident for something as bold as marriage. They thought I was walking on the aisle runner the usher had rolled out before I entered the sanctuary. I knew it was water. I knew it was the impossible. I knew God had brought me here and that as long as I held His hand He wouldn't let me drown, no matter how scary it got.

Preston took my hand and we stood. His face as bright as it had ever been and on mine was an answered prayer. Just six years before, I wouldn't have imagined a day like this. Where I would stand before a man and love him *really*, to say, "I do" and not despise the feel of it had to be a doing of God.

I knew the days after that day wouldn't all be a sugary thing. Some would be bitter. Others would bring new mercy. Either way, taking for myself a *selah* of this forever season called marriage, I approached it knowing it would be used of God to continue His work of sanctifying me and glorifying Himself.

From the outside looking in, it could be assumed that Preston's and my relationship was God's proof of turning a "gay girl good." But really, He'd already done that the moment He'd set me free from sin.

Marriage didn't "prove" that I'd changed. The fruit of the Spirit did (Galatians 5:22–23). The power to look at the things I'd loved once and conclude them as worthless was all of the apologetic that God needed to remind the world of His power.

Preston and I were brought together not so that we could become the standard of what is to become of all gay girls and boys turned believers. We were brought together for the primary reason of pointing to the mystery of God's gospel (Ephesians 5:32). Marriage was the way God wanted *me* to glorify Him. Becoming one flesh would not complete me. Marriage is not what would make me whole, but it would be God's work in and through my marriage, along with whatever else the Potter chose to use to shape me as His clay that would. God was my first love. I'd married Him way before I did Preston, and I'd be married to Him even after death parted me from the man I vowed to love until then.

CHAPTER 14

DO YOU BELIEVE IN miracles? Or a better question might be, do you believe that God still does impossible, unearthly kinds of things among us?

Perhaps you consider the miraculous a thing of the past. Something God did when Moses was alive. With blood inside of the Nile, instead of the salted water that left once Moses' staff touched the surface. Elijah knew for himself how unlimited God's power is when he begged Him to let a dead boy breathe again and watched it happen. Jonah wouldn't deny the various ways in which God's hand can make everything change colors. A suicide attempt still ended up as a rescue mission for both he and Nineveh. Grace sent a fish to carry him to shore and his voice to keep hundreds of thousands from drowning in wrath.

We saw the miraculous the most when Jesus showed up in the world, but He left awhile back, so maybe His miracles left the earth when He did? One thing is for sure: even when Jesus was around, doing what eyes had not seen, or ears had not heard, people still refused to believe.

One time in particular,[12] while passing the temple with His disciples, Jesus observed a man who'd been born blind. Being unable to see, the man couldn't recognize that Jesus was looking at him. But his ears must have picked up the sound of several feet walking toward him. Around this temple, it was dark always, at least to him. He knew the sun was out when he could feel the heat, taking advantage of the day and the worshipers that went for prayer during it, he begged them for help. He always ended up with less money than the number of feet he'd heard pass by, but surrounded by nothing but a sightless awareness of everything, he still sat there.

In what he could sense was in front of him, someone stood. By now, the sound of several falling coins would've clanked up and into his ear. An encouragement to his belly, for it was the sound of a meal to come.

But it was the wet noise of spit splitting the lips of the nearby body that focused both ears. The man shrunk back quickly—usually the sound of spit indicated the sound of javelin hurled from the throat of those who despised insignificants like him. Only, the spit landed in the dirt. The dirt was being

---

[12] John 9:1–34.

moved around now. What was happening? He didn't have the eyes to know, but Jesus was mixing His saliva in with the dirt and making mud out of it. He'd done something similar a long, long time before this, when the ground became the makings of a man. Here, the dirt would heal a man He'd made.

Whoever it was—the man standing, messing with the dirt around him—put what he now felt to be mud, sticky and smelling like spit, on his eyes. Before asking anything, the anonymous one finally said something. The blind man heard, "Go, wash in the pool of Siloam." The man's face was hidden by blindness but by the sound of His voice, He had to be important. Maybe even regal, but kings had long been gone from Israel and if one passed by, he wouldn't have paid any attention to the ground to recognize a beggar sitting on it. "Go." Sounded like "Obey." "Wash in the pool" sounded like "Here, now." So, having traveled to the nearby pool on occasion, he went. He followed the man's directions. Grabbing water with both hands, like two random ships sinking on purpose, and rubbing it against the mud. Throwing water on the left eye, the right eye, cleaning the mud off inconsistently, tasting some as it rolled into his mouth, he started to see it drip off his hands. Using his palms to brush the stubborn sections away from his eyelids, light startled him. As more mud fell, more sight came. Until at once, he could see.

Walking back toward the temple, people saw him seeing them. They were used to his eyes either being closed or wandering, unable to steady themselves on an object and see it plainly. He looked *at* them now, and they couldn't figure out if it was actually him or another man who had the same face but who had always had sight. Hearing *and* seeing them question if he was the same man known for begging blindly outside of the temple, he told them he was in fact the same man. When asked how then could he see, he told them how a man called Jesus did it. Eventually, the miracle was brought to the attention of the Pharisees who questioned the man just as the Jews did. They even asked his parents if when he was born to them, he came out of the womb an unseeing child. To which they confirmed he did. Now their son knew what his parents looked like, and Jesus was the One who did it.

The Pharisees could not fathom the thought that Jesus, a man claiming to be one with God, a Messiah dressed in carpenter's clothing, was the one who'd performed this miracle. Or even that the miracle was actual and not just hysteria. Blind men *stay* blind. Unless, the truth was that they had never been blind at all. And hypothetically, if their eyes had actually been opened, there was no way a Jewish man from Galilee had done it. Blinded by their commitment to unbelief, unwilling to look past the miracle to see the glory of God in it, they cast the now seeing man from their midst. But Jesus found him and asked, "Do you believe in the Son of Man?" "Who is He, Sir, that I may believe in Him?" he asked. Jesus answered, "You have *seen*

Him; in fact, He is the One speaking with you." "I believe, Lord!" he said, and he worshiped Him. Jesus said, "I came into this world for judgment, in order that those who do not see will see and those who do see will become blind."

Do you know why we have a hard time believing that a gay girl can become a completely different creature? Because, we have a hard time believing God. The Pharisees saw the man born blind, heard his testimony, heard about his past and how it was completely different from the present one, and refused to believe the miracle because of *Who* the miracle pointed to. They were skeptical of the miracle because they didn't have a real faith in the God who'd done it. The miracle was less about the blind man and more about a good God. It showed *Him* off. His power. His ability to do what He wants. How He wants, when He wants, and to whomever He chooses.

The incomprehensible nature of what Jesus had done, was to show all men that Jesus was indeed God in the flesh. And in being so, everything He said about Himself and the world was absolutely true. The miracle would be used by Jesus for future generations to reveal the great blindness in every man that is convinced of their own goodness. That somehow, they can succeed at life without Him. Walking throughout the world, blind as ever, believing that the darkness in which they spend all of their days is actually light.

Jesus came into the world to give sight, not only because He wanted to but also because He *could*. A miracle is called that for a reason. It is harder to lift the hardness off of the heart of a sinner than it is to give a blind man physical sight. Humans have been unable to open their own eyes, spiritually, since Adam hid behind the tree in hopes that his hiding from God could save him from God. We've all become very creative at trying to make ourselves see, but we will never succeed. God wouldn't be Himself if He could not do the impossible. Before time, He's done it, and when time becomes a distant memory used only to reminisce, He will always be doing what no one can: be God. The God who does the miraculous. And we can be sure that the salvation of a sinner is the greatest miracle the world could ever see.

The same power that made a man born blind able to see through the means of something as foolish as spit and mud is the same enormous power contained in a foolish gospel brought into the world through a risen Savior. It is through faith in Him, initiated by His pursuit of me, that I, a gay girl, now new creature, was made right with God. Given sight, able to recognize my hands and how they'd been calloused by sin, and how Jesus had come to cleanse me of them all. Now seeing, I worship. One thing is sure, if ever I am asked, how am I able to see now, after being blind for so long, I will simply say, "I was blind, a good God came, and now, I see."

PART 3

Same-Sex Attraction *AND* . . .

THESE CONCLUDING CHAPTERS ARE to be a resource. I've said a lot about me thus far, and about God, but if you're anything like me, you're wondering, *What now? Is there something practical that I can take hold of for myself or my friends or my coworkers?* And I believe this next section, though not exhaustive, can be of some use for you if so.

Throughout, I will make many references to "Same-Sex-Attracted Christians." Or for short, "SSA Christians." The use of the title is referring to born-again men and women who by grace through faith have repented of their sins (including homosexuality) and have placed their faith in the Lord Jesus Christ. These men and women are referred to as an SSA Christian because, though they have been renewed by the power of the Spirit, they are still tempted by the flesh to do what is displeasing to God, namely, to submit to all disordered versions of sexuality.

I only use the designation to be specific about to whom it is that I am speaking, or about, as it relates to the topic at hand. To be clear, I am not implying that because these men and women are still tempted with SSA, that they bear the identity of what some would call a "Gay Christian." Again, as I said before, I don't believe it is wise or truthful to the power of the gospel to identify oneself by the sins of one's past or the temptations of one's present but rather to only be defined by the Christ who's overcome both for those He calls His own. All men and women, including myself, that are well acquainted with sexual temptation are ultimately not what our temptation says of us. We are what Christ had done for us; therefore, our ultimate identity is very simple: We are Christians.

CHAPTER 15

Same-Sex Attraction and Identity

IDENTITY IS A BIG deal. It, like a language we carry on our faces, says a lot of what we believe about God, ourselves, and others. Unable to help itself, it will determine the "how" that governs our steps. The way we move about the world can always be traced back to the question, "Who am I today?" and "What is God always?" The question is one of incredible importance for born-again Christians that are yet and still SSA. The world we find ourselves in has made sexuality central to our identity. An identity where pride is demonstrated by waving a promise made after God destroyed the world with water. Gayness is not just a way to act but a way to *be*. It is, as they say, "Just who you are."

LGBT culture has done an excellent job of renewing or should I say, destroying, the mind of many, mainly by consistently using words as their greatest tool in their efforts to draw people into finding greater joy in identifying with their sin rather than their Creator. Once sanctification begins in the life of a believer that has SSA, mind renewal has also begun. A beautiful miracle in which God enters in and starts turning the heart into the cathedral it was intended to be. As the heart is, the mind is also. A new heart is the beginning of a new mind, but there is still effort needed on our end. We don't just sit back and expect great fruitfulness to come from minimal zeal. We work alongside God to "act the miracle" (see Philippians 2:12–13) of sanctification into its grandest potential.[13]

When a person, once enslaved to their SSA, becomes a believer, it can be difficult for them to learn how to identify themselves by another affection. Or, if not a problem of strain, then it can be one of ignorance. Someone must know that how they identify themselves will shape how they navigate life. In my own journey with God, I have seen the impact identity can have on my faith. When I begin to forget that I *am* loved, that I *am* forgiven, and that I *am* new—then I stop operating out of faith and instead start to behave as if my thoughts are more inerrant than the Scriptures. The identity I ascribe to God and the identity He gives me will always reveal the true nature of my faith.

So, the burden for SSA Christians—when it comes to identity—is not to learn more about themselves or to "become

---

[13] www.desiringgod.org/messages/i-act-the-miracle

a better you" as an entry into self-empowerment. It is to renew the mind so that men and women begin seeing themselves in light of who God has revealed Himself to be so that they can glorify Him in the ways He commanded. This happens among community, with much prayer, and with a consistent, thoughtful internalizing of the Word of God.

Below, are four categories that I believe will help the SSA believer as they "act the miracle" of sanctification as it relates to identity. Below each heading, you will find a list of Scriptures that I hope will, when read prayerfully, believed fully, and meditated on daily, assist SSA believers as they begin the journey of not being conformed to the world they were delivered from and are transformed by the renewal of their mind (Romans 12:2).

1. Identity of Sin | Sin is not beautiful.

First, when the identity of the heart changes, so must the identity of sin. While *in it*, the eyes only see it as a woman does a diamond ring. Or as a child does a gift, covered in wrapping waiting to be torn into confetti. Sin is attractive to sinners. But for saints, it must be stripped naked of its masks, pushed out into the light, and seen for what it is. The saint is new but their temptations will be as old as the devil. His tactics of enticement are not at all updated. From Eden until now, in pulling a person toward sin, he must first convince them that the thing for which they feel compelled to taste will be a satisfying one.

And in us, the doubt that we are born carrying moves up and into the sight as temptation dizzies us into wanting to believe the sin Christ nailed to the cross is only a bright red rose to be picked off and smelled for pleasure. Unbelief will always contrast sin with God. Making *it* and not Him glorious. Making *it* and not Him what makes life worth living. Making *it* and not Him worth dying for.

There will come a day or two or many for the SSA Christian when the affections for which they once delighted in will whisper for them to return. It will whisper the promise of joy and fulfillment. But it will *feel* more true than it is, for sin can never deliver on its promise to make us happy. Vomit will always be vomit even if drizzled with chocolate, sliced almonds, and a cherry on top (2 Peter 2:21–22). When the temptation to see sin as what it is not arrives, the Scriptures are our light, our final truth, our escape out of the shadow moving toward our feet. The Word of God and not the word of the enemy is where we see the *true* identity of sin.

> For the wages of sin is death. (Romans 6:23)

> But each person is tempted when he is lured and enticed by his own desire. Then desire when it has conceived gives birth to sin, and sin when it is fully grown brings forth death. (James 1:14–15)

But what fruit were you getting at that time from the things of which you are now ashamed? For the end of those things is death. (Romans 6:21)

There is a way that seems right to a man, but its end is the way to death. (Proverbs 14:12)

Do not love the world or the things in the world. If anyone loves the world, the love of the Father is not in him. (1 John 2:15)

Whoever makes a practice of sinning is of the devil, for the devil has been sinning from the beginning. (1 John 3:8)

They were filled with all manner of unrighteousness, evil, covetousness, malice. They are full of envy, murder, strife, deceit, maliciousness. They are gossips, slanderers, haters of God, insolent, haughty, boastful, inventors of evil, disobedient to parents, foolish, faithless, heartless, ruthless. Though they know God's righteous decree that those who practice such things deserve to die, they not only do them but give approval to those who practice them. (Romans 1:29–32)

All who fashion idols are nothing, and the things they delight in do not profit. Their witnesses neither see nor know, that they may be put to shame. (Isaiah 44:9)

Let not sin therefore reign in your mortal body, to make you obey its passions. Do not present your members to sin as instruments for unrighteousness, but present yourselves to God as those who have been brought from death to life, and your members to God as instruments for righteousness. (Romans 6:12–13)

2. Identity of a Saint | You are not your temptations.

Temptations talk, a lot. They tell us of their potential. They speak of our need and say they can fix it. When heard as often as the day changes colors, temptation brings with it a shame of a different dialect. The SSA Christian that resists out of habit can start to get a ragged ear, unraveled by the long-winded nature of the temptations they can't help but hear. Shame doesn't replace the other voice; they work in tandem. One louder than the other depending on the identity the SSA Christian starts to let cover their joy.

Shame wants us to believe it is accurate in its evaluation of us. That we are too wretched to be made new. Too dirty to be made clean. Too prone to sin for forgiveness to matter. That in all the fruits of the great salvation we've come to bear, that the temptation to still *want* our gay exes or to feel how it felt to be loved by someone of the same sex, means that we are just a sinner beyond repair or worse, that we are simply *still gay*. But just because we are tempted does not mean that we *are* our temptations.

We are what the cross has declared us to be: forgiven. Temptations may have a voice but so does the Living God. The Scriptures—God breathed and eternally profitable—have the final say on the identity of the saint.

> Or do you not know that the unrighteous will not inherit the kingdom of God? Do not be deceived: neither the sexually immoral, nor idolaters, nor adulterers, nor men who practice homosexuality, nor thieves, nor the greedy, nor drunkards, nor revilers, nor swindlers will inherit the kingdom of God. And such were some of you. But you were washed, you were sanctified, you were justified in the name of the Lord Jesus Christ and by the Spirit of our God. (1 Corinthians 6:9–11)
>
> Therefore, if anyone is in Christ, he is a new creation. The old has passed away; behold, the new has come. (2 Corinthians 5:17)
>
> But now that you have been set free from sin and have become slaves of God, the fruit you get leads to sanctification and its end, eternal life. (Romans 6:22)
>
> In love he predestined us for adoption to himself as sons through Jesus Christ, according to the purpose of his will,

to the praise of his glorious grace, with which he has blessed us in the Beloved. (Ephesian 1:4–6)

For we are his workmanship, created in Christ Jesus for good works, which God prepared beforehand, that we should walk in them. (Ephesians 2:10)

Who is to condemn? Christ Jesus is the one who died—more than that, who was raised—who is at the right hand of God, who indeed is interceding for us. (Romans 8:34)

My little children, I am writing these things to you so that you may not sin. But if anyone does sin, we have an advocate with the Father, Jesus Christ the righteous. (1 John 2:1)

There is therefore now no condemnation for those who are in Christ Jesus. (Romans 8:1)

But to all who did receive him, who believed in his name, he gave the right to become children of God, who were born, not of blood nor of the will of the flesh nor of the will of man, but of God. (John 1:12–13)

Therefore, since we have been justified by faith, we have peace with God through our Lord Jesus Christ. Through him we have also obtained access by faith into this grace

in which we stand, and we rejoice in hope of the glory of
God. (Romans 5:1–2)

No, in all these things we are more than conquerors
through him who loved us. For I am sure that neither
death nor life, nor angels nor rulers, nor things present
nor things to come, nor powers, nor height nor depth,
nor anything else in all creation, will be able to sepa-
rate us from the love of God in Christ Jesus our Lord.
(Romans 8:37–39)

3. Identity of the Church | You are not alone.

Being an SSA Christian can *seem* like a solitary walk. One
foot in front of the other without the echo of another pair of
legs to share the sound of movement with. There is the fear of
being misunderstood, judged, unloved, or accepted fully. When
in a room full of believers, the past is a letter made of scarlet
between eyes, the isolation imagined to be more present than
bodies discourages the Christian into assuming themselves
alone. Loneliness being their destined identity. Others conclude that they can succeed at the Christian faith without the
presence of other Christians. That they can be a single soldier
in the battle against sin, the devil, and the flesh, outnumbered
unknowingly, they haven't the foresight to see that no war has
been won alone. Or the wisdom to gather that sanctification is
as communal as communion. You are not alone.

Both, the isolated Christian and the isolating Christian are a part of a family, a body, an organism of human beings with different sins and the same Savior. Even if many Christians cannot understand the specific struggle of SSA, all Christians can understand the general struggle of sin. It is this body that God has made us all a part of to sanctify the saints, equip the saints for ministry, and reveal God in deeper ways to the saints. It was true then, and it is true now, that man was not meant to be alone. And by the grace of God, we are not and will never be.

> So then you are no longer strangers and aliens, but you are fellow citizens with the saints and members of the household of God, built on the foundation of the apostles and prophets, Christ Jesus himself being the cornerstone, in whom the whole structure, being joined together, grows into a holy temple in the Lord. In him you also are being built together into a dwelling place for God by the Spirit. (Ephesians 2:19–22)

> But you are a chosen race, a royal priesthood, a holy nation, a people for his own possession, that you may proclaim the excellencies of him who called you out of darkness into his marvelous light. (1 Peter 2:9)

> Where there is no guidance, a people falls, but in an abundance of counselors there is safety. (Proverbs 11:14)

But exhort one another every day, as long as it is called "today," that none of you may be hardened by the deceitfulness of sin. (Hebrews 3:13)

And let us consider how to stir up one another to love and good works, not neglecting to meet together, as is the habit of some, but encouraging one another, and all the more as you see the Day drawing near. (Hebrews 10:24–25)

Rather, speaking the truth in love, we are to grow up in every way into him who is the head, into Christ, from whom the whole body, joined and held together by every joint with which it is equipped, when each part is working properly, makes the body grow so that it builds itself up in love. (Ephesians 4:15–16)

If one member suffers, all suffer together; if one member is honored, all rejoice together. (1 Corinthians 12:26)

After this I looked, and behold, a great multitude that no one could number, from every nation, from all tribes and peoples and languages, standing before the throne and before the Lamb, clothed in white robes, with palm branches in their hands, and crying out with a loud voice, "Salvation belongs to our God who sits on the throne, and to the Lamb!" (Revelation 7:9–10)

4. Identity of God | God is better than you can imagine.

The root of all sin is unbelief in God. The fall began when Adam and Eve doubted what God said about Himself. It is the identity that we ascribe to God out of doubt or faith in His Scriptures that will determine the identity we will give ourselves and ultimately the life that we inevitably live. If He is the Creator, then we are created. If He is Master, then we are servants. If He is love, then we are loved. If He is omnipotent, then we are not as powerful as we think. If He is omniscient, then there is nowhere to hide. If He cannot lie, then His promises are all true. It is faith in the truths of God's character that has the power to completely revolutionize how our lives are lived out. Not only that, there is so much joy to be had on Earth because there is more glory in God than we can imagine.

He is so much greater than the greatest thing and much more glorious than the most glorious glory the eyes could see. Knowing this, He becomes the aim of all of our doing. Because, if God is bigger than we can imagine, we are wasting our time to chase after something or someone lesser than Him. And because we know that He is our all in all, in our temptations, our trials, and our victories, we must place our ultimate identity not in who we are, but in who we know God to be.

*Have you not known? Have you not heard? The L*ORD *is the everlasting God, the Creator of the ends of the earth. He does not faint or grow weary; his understanding is unsearchable. He gives power to the faint, and to him who has no might he increases strength. Even youths shall faint and be weary, and young men shall fall exhausted; but they who wait for the L*ORD *shall renew their strength; they shall mount up with wings like eagles, they shall run and not be weary; they shall walk and not faint. (Isaiah 40:28–31)*

*The L*ORD *is gracious and merciful, slow to anger and abounding in steadfast love. The L*ORD *is good to all, and his mercy is over all that he has made. (Psalm 145:8–9)*

You make known to me the path of life; in your presence there is fullness of joy; at your right hand are pleasures forevermore. (Psalm 16:11)

*"But let him who boasts boast in this, that he understands and knows me, that I am the L*ORD *who practices steadfast love, justice, and righteousness in the earth. For in these things I delight, declares the L*ORD*." (Jeremiah 9:24)*

To whom then will you liken God, or what likeness compare with him? (Isaiah 40:18)

In the year that King Uzziah died I saw the Lord sitting upon a throne, high and lifted up; and the train of his robe filled the temple. Above him stood the seraphim. Each had six wings: with two he covered his face, and with two he covered his feet, and with two he flew. And one called to another and said: "Holy, holy, holy is the LORD of hosts; the whole earth is full of his glory!" (Isaiah 6:1–3)

Behold, the LORD's hand is not shortened, that it cannot save, or his ear dull, that it cannot hear. (Isaiah 59:1)

Then he rose and rebuked the winds and the sea, and there was a great calm. And the men marveled, saying, "What sort of man is this, that even winds and seas obey him?" (Matthew 8:26–27)

He himself bore our sins in his body on the tree, that we might die to sin and live to righteousness. By his wounds you have been healed. (1 Peter 2:24)

We love because he first loved us. (1 John 4:19)

He is the image of the invisible God, the firstborn of all creation. For by him all things were created, in heaven and on earth, visible and invisible, whether thrones or dominions or rulers or authorities—all things were created through him and for him. And he is before all things, and in him all things hold together. And he is the head of the body, the church. He is the beginning, the firstborn from the dead, that in everything he might be preeminent. For in him all the fullness of God was pleased to dwell, and through him to reconcile to himself all things, whether on earth or in heaven, making peace by the blood of his cross. (Colossians 1:15–20)

And being found in human form, he humbled himself by becoming obedient to the point of death, even death on a cross. Therefore God has highly exalted him and bestowed on him the name that is above every name, so that at the name of Jesus every knee should bow, in heaven and on earth and under the earth, and every tongue confess that Jesus Christ is Lord, to the glory of God the Father. (Philippians 2:8–11)

Now to him who is able to keep you from stumbling and to present you blameless before the presence of his glory with great joy, to the only God, our Savior, through Jesus Christ our Lord, be glory, majesty, dominion, and authority, before all time and now and forever. Amen. (Jude 24–25)

And he who was seated on the throne said, "Behold, I am making all things new." Also he said, "Write this down, for these words are trustworthy and true." And he said to me, "It is done! I am the Alpha and the Omega, the beginning and the end. To the thirsty I will

give from the spring of the water of life without pay-
ment." (Revelation 21:5–6)

It should be an *expectation* of both newer and older
believers coming out of the LGBT community that they will
experience the temptation to identify as something other
than what Scripture has declared as true. Whether it is the
identity of sin, the identity of the saint, the identity of the
church or the identity of God, there is a real enemy that
takes delight in our doubt. But the greatest weapon we have
against him and even our own flesh is faith in God's Word.
By trusting it as having the final say, we will remain strong
even when we are weak.

Be encouraged.

> Finally, be strong in the Lord and in the strength
> of his might. Put on the whole armor of God, that
> you may be able to stand against the schemes of
> the devil. For we do not wrestle against flesh and
> blood, but against the rulers, against the authori-
> ties, against the cosmic powers over this present
> darkness, against the spiritual forces of evil in
> the heavenly places. Therefore take up the whole
> armor of God, that you may be able to withstand
> in the evil day, and having done all, to stand firm.
> Stand therefore, having fastened on the belt of

truth, and having put on the breastplate of righteousness, and, as shoes for your feet, having put on the readiness given by the gospel of peace. In all circumstances take up the shield of faith, with which you can extinguish all the flaming darts of the evil one; and take the helmet of salvation, and the sword of the Spirit, which is the word of God, praying at all times in the Spirit, with all prayer and supplication. (Ephesians 6:10–18)

CHAPTER 16

Same-Sex Attraction and Endurance

ENDURANCE, FOR SOME STRANGE reason, is an uncommon word, especially in conversations centered around same-sex attraction. Maybe, in a culture where "quick" is preferred over "wait," and "easy" over "difficult," it's to be expected then that a discussion regarding enduring, powerful, sometimes unrelenting, temptation of same-sex attraction would only be occasional. As odd as it may be to some, it is intrinsic to the Christian experience, and the refusal to employ it as a weapon of faith would ensure that the professing Christian will not persevere (Matthew 24:13).

I've had countless conversations with many same-sex attracted men and women who are either trying to adhere to a biblical sexual ethic or have tried. Weary-eyed and burdened, they come to me, head almost bowed, to welcome me into their frustration. Eventually, they confess the reason for their cloudiness: "It's just so hard," they say. Leaving the sentence without any extra explanation. The difficulty of trying to resist SSA tends to lead some into the depressing cycle of self-condemnation and discouragement. For others, it can lead them away from the faith they once attempted to anchor themselves in all together.

I've always wondered if when they became a disciple, or thought themselves to be one, if they knew that following Jesus not only meant eternal life but also a crucified one. Crucifixions were not only excruciating (a word derived from crucifixion itself) but they were slow. A long, sun-setting-more-than-once kind of death. Being crucified made certain that death would arrive, but when it chose to cut short, the bloody waiting depended on time. Being disconnected from the historical understanding of crucifixion as it relates to time and not just pain may be the reason for our partial grasp of Jesus' words in Luke 9:23: "If anyone would come after me, let him deny himself and take up his cross daily and follow me." We know this verse means dying to self, but how often have we seen in it the kind of patient, daily, drawn-out dying that will come of wearing our own cross. That once nailed to our back, it will by no means mean that the sin we die to today will not return tomorrow for us to put it to death again and again until after a season or a lifetime, we discover it dead, finally. The crucified life is the life set on enduring until the end when once and for all, the cross is replaced with a crown.

For the SSA Christian, Jesus modeled the difficult (yet possible) work of enduring for the glory of God when the body would rather retreat. In Matthew 26, we find Him headed toward Gethsemane. He'd just eaten a meal with His disciples, and afterward He brought them to one of His favorite places to pray. For the time was coming for Him to do what He'd come to do. Die.

The plan was for Him to speak with the God whose voice He's known before the sky heard it split the day from night. The sun gone, their bellies full of Passover lamb, bread, and wine, body fatigued from walking, they are tired, yet Jesus commands them to do something other than rest. He wants them to watch. Sleep, though natural, was not what they needed. To keep their eyes open and awake to the temptations on the way was the requirement of the moment.

Walking a short distance from them, Jesus' body spoke before He did. It landed face-first, breathing into the grass, back, upward, and under stars, and moon lit with all sorts of sorrow—the posture of someone who's too desperate to stand. Prostrate, He addresses God by name, followed by asking of Him what none other than He could grant, "My Father, if it be possible, let this cup pass from me" (Matthew 26:39). This cup being a symbol, a picture, a metaphor for the wrath of God.

This was another type of drowning earth, with a distant ark. A duplicate sulfur and fire from heaven set to fall on a Son instead of Sodom this time. A forty-year wilderness shrunken and squeezed into one restless night, from which the Son could find no Sabbath. This cup held in it nothing Jesus had ever tasted. He'd only known the pleasure of God in Him and the love of God for Him (Matthew 3:17; John 5:20). The agony of the cross from which He wanted to escape, if possible, was not primarily the physical pain to come, but the experience of being an enemy of His Father—because of the sin He would carry on our behalf. And if it were possible, He didn't want to do it, at least in *this* way.

There is no other way to please God except to obey by faith. Obedience for those who are SSA deals in the terrifying because it means to deny the body of what often feels as natural as smiling. SSA is usually not concocted or becoming of a particular imagination. It's a real affection experienced by real people. So when commanded not to act out on these affections, even when they pulse through the body loud enough to make a sound, it takes an unearthly commitment to self-denial. Many will hesitantly but willing take on the challenge, until they notice that such a task is not an easy one.

But usually, they crescendo into a steady string of temptations that return just as quick as they were put to death. Frustration and discouragement leads some into considering unbelief and all that it has to say about what they are to do. Unbelief, just like Satan, will always take the easy way out. It will tell us to eat the fruit in exchange for knowledge, instead of fearing God to gain real wisdom. Unbelief will unravel our perceptions of both suffering and the blessedness of life and beckon us to skip self-denial at all costs with the faux promises of comfort that can't extend beyond the grave. And for so many others, unbelief has convinced them that they can serve both God and homosexuality. Both God and flesh. Both sin and Savior. For this, we know, is impossible. "No one born of God makes a practice of sinning, for God's seed abides in him; and he cannot keep on sinning, because he has been born of God" (1 John 3:9). The Christian that deals with SSA should never look for another way to obey God that is outside of the will of God. For we know that just as it was His will for Jesus to be crucified, it is also His will for all to abstain from all forms of sexuality that are not in accordance with His Scriptures. "For this is the will of God, your sanctification: that you abstain from sexual immorality" (1 Thessalonians 4:3).

If there was another way to go about obeying the will of God, Jesus wanted that option but there was only ONE way. And He was completely committed to it. He, still bowed toward the earth, says to His Father, ". . . nevertheless, not as I will, but as you will." Jesus asks His Father if the cup could pass from Him three different times. And as if silence was interesting, that's all Jesus heard in response. Neither the wind wrapped Him up and gave Him a piece of God's mind nor did the mount He laid on shake the heavens into a familiar voice. In all of His agony, God said nothing.

Someone might wonder if in God's choosing not to speak, whether He might have at least decided to act. And He did. He sent an angel from heaven. But the angel was not sent for the trivial reasons we'd all expect of other fathers who might be more committed to the comfort of their child than to the glory of God's name. The angel God sent didn't come to gather up the depressed Son of God and carry Him back to heaven before the cross. If needed, one angel could've come with tens of thousands of others to find and finish all of Jesus' enemies. This, of course, would at least make the long walk to Calvary easier for the Christ, but this too was not the agenda of God. If only the angel had come to deliver Jesus from every fear, anxiety, pain, sorrow, difficulty, temptation, or whatever else His body had to carry; but His Father did something completely different than deliver His Son into ease. Not allowing Jesus to skip the adversity of obedience, He sent the angel to simply strengthen the Son so that He could endure it.

If Jesus needed the strength to endure for the sake of obedience to His Father, how much more do we? Even the writer of Hebrews understood the believer's need for perseverance when he wrote, "Therefore do not throw away your confidence, which has a great reward. For you have need of endurance, so that when you have done the will of God you may receive what is promised" (Hebrews 10:35–36). The fact of the matter is, being a Christian and having to deny SSA is difficult (difficult is an understatement), but just as the Father sent an angel to strengthen the Son, He has sent us someone way better: the Holy Spirit. It is when we are led by the Spirit, as we look to Jesus and not discouragement (or lies or condemnation) that we are able to do what pleases the Father. Being strengthened to endure and being given the power to obey doesn't make obedience easy, but it does make it possible.

There is something to be said of love in all of this. If the Garden of Gethsemane had been told differently, something like an inverted form of this familiar gospel narrative, I imagine it would stretch Jesus into someone more human than holy. What if, after having Passover dinner with His disciples, Jesus enters the garden to pray. Instead of having a body heavy enough to need God, He stands still. Still with indifference to the flaming clouds on their way to snatch His own light from the earth. He speaks with the Father as intended, but no blood falls out of His head. As a person with no grief would pray, He does so too. No petitions. No agony. No depression. No deep, soul-beg to God for His cup to pass. This cup He knows will come down on Him, in all of its wrath, stored up and ready to pour. But, there is no sign of wanting to escape what will spill out. Or even if what is to come has registered to Him as a terrible thing. He is calm. As if the crucifixion will just be a regular ol' day.

If this were the version of Jesus we were to read instead, what would it say about love, His love for God, that is? It would say that Jesus might not have loved God as much as we thought He did. If when the time was coming for Him to experience the full vengeance of God instead of the sweet love in which He'd always abided, He approached it with indifference, we could only conclude that He didn't care *that much* about having His intimacy with the Father disrupted. But the true story is that Jesus *did* care. He cared to the point of utter misery, which shook the blood from His body and the petitions from His heart. It is the great agony that we see in Jesus as He endured that reveals to us His unimaginable love for His Father. He would rather the cup pass than to not abide in this love.

The great contrast between us and Jesus is this: Jesus was sorrowful at the prospect of Him experiencing the displeasure of God, but most, if not all, of us become sorrowful at the prospect of not experiencing the pleasures of sin.

Jesus didn't endure because He was strong; He was most likely at one of the weakest points of His humanity, but He endured because He loved His God. Therefore, He was fully committed to doing the will of God, no matter the cost. This love is what will help us persevere: a love that sees knowing God as the body's greatest pleasure.

Even in tears, and pain, and difficulty, we keep fighting because we know being in His will is infinitely better than being in our own. And just like Jesus, we endure because we know joy will always be on the other side of obedience. So we look to Him, "The founder and perfecter of our faith, who for the joy that was set before him endured the cross, despising the shame, and is seated at the right hand of the throne of God" (Hebrews 12:2).

CHAPTER 17

Same-Sex Attraction and the
Heterosexual Gospel

GOD ISN'T CALLING GAY people to be straight.

You'd think He was by listening to the ways Christians try to encourage same-sex-attracted people within, or outside, their local churches. They dangle the possibility of heterosexual marriage above their heads, point to it like it's heaven on a string, something to grab and get whole with. And though it's usually well-meaning, it's very dangerous. Why? Because it puts more emphasis on marriage as the goal of the Christian life than knowing Jesus. Just as God's aim in my salvation was not mainly the removal of my same-sex desires, in sanctification, it is not always His aim that marriage or experiencing an attraction for the opposite sex will be involved.

The "heterosexual gospel" is one that encourages SSA men and women to come to Jesus so that they *can* be straight or that coming to Jesus ensures that they *will* be sexually attracted to the opposite sex. The ways in which this "gospel" is preached is much more subtle than I've made it out to be. It usually sounds like, "I know you're struggling with being gay. I can promise you, if you give your life to Jesus, He will completely deliver you from those desires because He loves you," or "I know a guy that used to be gay and now he's married. Jesus will do the same for you if you trust Him." God surely can deliver someone completely of SSA and God definitely can take an SSA man or woman and turn them into a spouse to the opposite sex (I'm obviously a witness of that), but the Scriptures have not explicitly promised these as definitive gifts for being reconciled to God, or as the immediate inherited blessing of regeneration. In hopes of encouraging SSA individuals and those who are seeking to love them well, here are four reasons to avoid the heterosexual gospel:

1. We are more than our sexuality.

So God created man in his own image, in the image of God he created him; male and female he created them. (Genesis 1:27)

We are all much more complex than we know. We were made differently than the rest of creation. We were created with a mind that bends depending on where the eyes land. Looking around, you'll see how colorful feelings can be. We are intellectual, emotional, and spiritual beings. We possess the capacity for joy, sadness, pride, humility, terror, and safety, all working together with our souls as humans. This then is why limiting our personhood to sexuality is a shortsighted way to describe how God has made us. Being made in His image, we were made to love Him, not out of an animal instinct, but with our human wills—involving the heart, mind, and soul. When God is not loved by our entire being, sin is exposed by how we speak, create, and think—what we do with our bodies, and how we treat others, in what we choose for our ears to hear and our eyes to watch, etc. Therefore, our sexuality may be a *part* of who we are, but it is not *all* that we are. Humans are more than who they are sexually attracted to.

God is triune, being so much bigger than our minds have the capacity to understand. He is one God, in three persons, Father, Son, and Holy Spirit, all able to feel, act, listen, in unified and distinct ways from the other. This being the case, wouldn't it stand to reason that those He created in His image are similarly diverse and complex? If He made the *whole* person, then you can be sure that He wants to save and satisfy the *whole* person with Himself.

What could be implied from those who preach the "heterosexual gospel" is that our sexuality is all that God cares about. I am convinced that this thinking has kept many SSA men and women from experiencing the beauty of true repentance.

I realized this one day while interacting with a young lady who was offended by my testimony of overcoming homosexuality. After a few personal attacks and curse words, I asked her this question, "Let's just say homosexuality wasn't even an issue for you. Would God still be pleased with your life as a whole?" To which she responded, mildly caught off guard by the angle of my question, "Nah. Nah, He wouldn't." I asked her that question, specifically, because I needed her to see that God had more than her sexual actions in mind when He commanded her (and us) to repent and believe the gospel of Jesus Christ. If we are as complex as He's made us to be, then surely we are much more sinful then we can imagine. And for that reason, when God comes to restore, He must do it entirely.

For the unbeliever that is SSA, God is not mainly calling them to be straight; He's calling them to Himself. To know Christ, love Christ, serve Christ, honor Christ, and exalt Christ, forever. When He is the aim of their repentance, and the object of their faith, they are made right with God the Father and given the power by the Holy Spirit to deny *all* sin—sexual and otherwise. Someone trying to pursue heterosexuality and not holiness is just as far from right standing with God as someone actively pursuing homosexuality. And in fact, when an SSA Christian pursues heterosexuality as the goal instead of Christ, they will ultimately find themselves merely replacing one idol for the other. Through abiding in Him and walking in the holiness that no one can see without the Lord (Hebrews 12:14), SSA Christians, even when alive to same-sex temptations, are able to choose God over their previous sexual identity. Their identity as image-bearers, and not their sexual impulses, is the primary identifier that many SSA men and women desperately need to hear from the pulpits and the pews. If sexuality was their (and our) primary identity, then that would make sexuality our primary call. But we were not ultimately made for sex; we were made for God and His glory alone (Col. 1:16).

2. Marriage is not the pinnacle of the Christian faith.

> Then I heard what seemed to be the voice of a great multitude, like the roar of many waters and like the sound of mighty peals of thunder, crying out, "Hallelujah! For the Lord our God the Almighty reigns. Let us rejoice and exult and give him the glory, for the marriage of the Lamb has come and his Bride has made herself ready; it was granted her to clothe herself with fine linen, bright and pure"—for the fine linen is the righteous deeds of the saints. And the angel said to me, "Write this: Blessed are those who are invited to the marriage supper of the Lamb." (Revelation 19:6–9)

Marriage is glorious. By design, it was meant to be so—a mysterious plan of God that points to the gospel (Ephesians 5). One man, one woman, two different people, who, under God are made one flesh. These two contrasting bodies share their time, thoughts, rooms, beds, and as fickle as it was, they share their love too. Handing it out in portions as obedience and trust snatches it from the heart to give away. It took a whole Old Testament worth of time to go by before this mystery was explained to the world. Once Jesus had come, died, rose, and sent the Holy Ghost to keep us, we were told how this whole marriage thing was more than we'd imagined it to be. That it had more to do with God than anything. That it was a breathing parable of Christ and His church. Christ being God in the flesh. His church being those of us sheep who heard His voice one day and followed our Shepherd into life. If the world needed a dim image of how Christ loved the church, they only needed to watch a man love and lead His wife over dinner. Submission, modeled by the church in Her submission to Christ could be seen when a wife loved her God enough to submit to her husband alone (Ephesians 5). As crazy as it sounds, God has given humans, who've made a covenant before God and man, the blessed chance of playing out the gospel in their homes daily. Marriage truly is glorious.

In all of its glory however, it is not the highest glory. Marriage, for some time, has been esteemed idealistically—as a mini-heaven perhaps, unguarded by golden gates, entered into preferably before a woman's pretty begins to die, or by the time a man is ready to plant his seed. From the time a young girl learns of love, she's taught it's in its purest form when a white dress carries a woman into an "I do." Cartoons and children's books indoctrinate us young with this ideal, but they aren't the only ones making a utopia out of marriage. Christians (sometimes unknowingly) continue to make it an undue part of their gospel witness to the SSA men and women of the world (and single heterosexual men and women). The exaggerated promise of marriage or the unbalanced emphasis on its place in the Christian life can lead SSA men and women to being disoriented about God's specific call for *them*. Which we can say with confidence God's call is this: to love God and love people (Matthew 22:36–40).

For some, loving God will lead them down a path of God-honoring marriage. For others, a life of God-exalting singleness. The SSA Christian that is called to marriage is no more of an apologetic for the power of God than the SSA Christian that is called to singleness. In both, God is glorified.

The book of Genesis introduced us to the mystery of marriage, and Revelation concludes with the consummation of what marriage reveals. In Revelation, we are given a glimpse of what will happen once the church, Christ's bride, forgiven sinners, stainless saints are finally at home with their Bridegroom, who purchased their "I do" when He declared, "It is finished." This is the highest glory of the Christian life, to be married to the King of Glory. Marriage is glorious, but it is not *Him*. Though many have projected onto marriage what only God can give in Himself, it is not God. It is a creation of God for the glory of

God so that the world can get a picture of the gospel of God. Beyond Earth, another trait setting marriage apart from the Lord Himself is that it is not eternal. It will expire once the breath does and become something done only on the earth until that itself is done anew. The marriage that will last, however, is the marriage between Christ and His church. Like two deathless stars meant to burn forever, God and His church will always be married. Always be in love. Always be One. So much so that death will never part them, for even that will be no more.

If it will be that earthly marriage will not last into eternity, then we cannot preach a "gospel" that makes it out to be something worth dying for. Earthly marriage is momentary; the church's marriage to Christ is forever.

3. Singleness is not a curse.

> I want you to be free from anxieties. The unmarried man is anxious about the things of the Lord, how to please the Lord. But the married man is anxious about worldly things, how to please his wife, and his interests are divided. And the unmarried or betrothed woman is anxious about the things of the Lord, how to be holy in body and spirit. But the married woman is anxious about worldly things, how to please her husband. I say this for your own benefit, not to lay any restraint upon you, but to promote good order and to secure your undivided devotion to the Lord. (1 Corinthians 7:32–35)

In the "heterosexual gospel," singleness is whispered or completely kept from the discussion of what might come after coming to faith in Christ. Singleness is that country no one wants other people to visit. So they rip the shape of its borders off of maps thinking that the possibility of its discovery might turn SSA travelers back around and into a darker continent. But countless SSA men and women deserve the privilege of having another passport if necessary.

It could be that in an attempt not to discourage SSA believers, Christians refrain from mentioning singleness as the only proper alternative for their lives *if* marriage never arrives. But honestly, to only mention marriage, and not include single-ness, is just as discouraging, if not more discouraging, for many dealing with SSA. Some SSA men and women haven't and will never fully know how it feels to have a sexual attraction for someone of the opposite sex. Though sexual attraction/desire is not the foundation for a fruitful heterosexual marriage, it is in fact an aspect of it. For these men and women, to be married would be more of a trial for them than a gift. But if they have no idea of the beauty of singleness because it was never presented to them on those terms, then how would they know to embrace the season for which they may find themselves in, with joy instead of despair.

There are many blessings to be found in the life of a single man or woman. Primarily, the glory of having a singular focus on how to please the Lord, and not the same worries that accompany married folks and busies their days. If seasonal, or for a lifetime, they have undistracted eyes that may be attentive to the Scriptures, devoted to prayer, to worship, and to community. When married, these become a juggling act of priorities. A walk in the park is like walking on water. This is not to say that singleness comes with ease, as we know the desire for sexual intimacy will persist, even as they resist the temptations that will come. But we are not to ignore the gospel's power to keep singles satisfied by mistakenly presenting marriage as being all-sufficient. We instead acknowledge the reality of wanting sexual/relational intimacy by pointing to the day when all desires will find their ultimate fulfillment in Christ.

It means singleness, like marriage, has a unique way of testifying to the gospel of grace. Jesus said there will be no marriage in the new creation. In that respect we'll be like the angels, neither marrying nor being given in marriage (Matt. 22:30). We will have the reality; we will no longer need the signpost.

By foregoing marriage now, singleness is a way of both anticipating this reality and testifying to its goodness. It's a way of saying this future reality is so certain that we can live according to it now. If marriage shows us the shape of the

gospel, singleness shows us its sufficiency. It's a
way of declaring to a world obsessed with sexual
and romantic intimacy that these things are not
ultimate, and that in Christ we possess what is.[14]
—Sam Allberry

As encouraging SSA Christians to see singleness as a gift
becomes common, our local church communities will need to
reevaluate the ways in which they have failed to be the family
of God to all, married and single, as God has called us to be.
The world sees romantic/sexual intimacy as the *only* real and
deep level of intimacy for people to experience. Therefore, the
call to singleness can be assumed to be a call to loneliness. We
know loneliness has never been the intention of God for His
image-bearers (Gen. 2:18). He, a triune God, is by nature a communal God and He has created us all to be communal as He is.
The problem is that for some singles, the feelings of loneliness
are so tangible because the presence of community is not. If we
are to help SSA singles know the well-deep non-sexual intimacy that can exist, the church must actively pursue to show it.

As long as this is the case culturally, and as long as
it's reflected in our churches, it will be very hard for
any single person to feel as though the Christian

---

[14] https://www.thegospelcoalition.org/article/how-celibacy
-can-fulfill-your-sexuality/

sexual ethic is plausible. So we need to make sure our church family really is a family. Jesus promises that "no one who has left home or brothers or sisters or mother or father or children or fields for me and the gospel will fail to receive a hundred times as much in this present age: homes, brothers, sisters, mothers, children and fields—along with persecutions—and in the age to come eternal life." So it should be the case that anyone who has joined our churches is able to say they've experienced an increase in intimacy and community.[15]

—Christopher Yuan

Though the "heterosexual gospel" may frame singleness as something unsightly and to be avoided, we know that even our Lord Jesus was a single man on Earth. Not lacking anything, but fully alive in the love and sustaining power of His Father. I do not doubt that as our Great High Priest, He is not only able to empathize with SSA singles in their general weaknesses but also in the specific weaknesses that might arise out of their singleness (Heb. 4:15–16). Even in weakness, in Him, they are made strong. Even in singleness, in Him, they are made whole.

[15] https://www.9marks.org/article/singleness-same-sex-attraction-and-the-church-a-conversation-with-sam-allberry-rosaria-butterfield-and-christopher-yuan/grea

4. Evangelism is about God.

For I delivered to you as of first importance what I also received: that Christ died for our sins in accordance with the Scriptures, that he was buried, that he was raised on the third day in accordance with the Scriptures. (1 Corinthians 15:3–4)

For I am not ashamed of the gospel, for it is the power of God for salvation to everyone who believes. (Romans 1:16)

For what we proclaim is not ourselves, but Jesus Christ as Lord, with ourselves as your servants for Jesus' sake. (2 Corinthians 4:5)

Evangelism is a word that means to share the good news—more specifically, in this case, the good news of the gospel. And this evangelism is all about God because the gospel is all about God. It is God who created us. God who we all sinned against. It is God who loved us. God who sent His Son Christ to Earth. It is Christ who lived the life that we couldn't. It is Christ who died that death that we deserve. It is Christ who appeased God's wrath. It is Christ that rose from the dead. It is Christ who sent His promised Holy Spirit. It is the Holy Spirit that unveils our eyes to see the glory of Christ. It is the Holy Spirit who softens our hardened hearts so that we will repent. It is Christ who we are commanded to place our faith in. It is Christ who saves us and it is Christ that gives us eternal life.

The most alarming problem with the "heterosexual gospel" is that it is no gospel at all. Its missionaries carry into the world a message unable to save and set free. It points to marriage or a temptation-less heterosexuality as the reason to repent or the fruit of repentance. The reason to turn from sin has *always* been so we can turn toward Jesus. I don't doubt that it's easy to mistake the heterosexual gospel for the gospel of God because many have forgotten that the gospel is actually about God in the first place. When the Christian life has become a practice in doing everything else but making Jesus known, what would we expect of our gospel presentations? They will naturally result in the telling of something empty and void of power—more moral than anything and sufficient to make men and women believe that they can be saved by and for some other means than Jesus.

Getting back to the foundational call of making God the center of our churches, our conversations, our doctrines, and our lives will ensure that He won't be left out of our evangelism. Surely, no man who has made God small in his own life will have the Godward focus to make Him big in their ministry to others.

Christ has simply come to make us right with God. And in making us right with God, He is satisfying us *in* God. Our sexuality is not our soul, marriage is not heaven, and singleness is not hell. So may we all preach the news that is good for a reason. For it proclaims to the world that Jesus has come so that all sinners, same-sex-attracted and opposite-sex-attracted, can be forgiven of their sins to love God and enjoy Him forever.

Afterword

Come and hear, all you who fear God, and I will tell
what he has done for my soul. (Psalm 66:16)

I WONDER WHY THE psalmist said it. Why he invited us to
listen in on something as wonderful as that. He could've kept
it all to himself and only told the favorite few he knew would
understand. Some stories are kept, tucked, and hidden from
plain sight. Brought out by force or choice, but he chose to tell
us despite what this telling might do to whoever decided to
listen. He made the decision to not withhold from us what happened to his soul, for it was too good to keep as the beginning
of a prayer. The kind that began with "I praise You because . . ."
and ended without sound. Silence is what can happen to the
mouth when the mind remembers grace and how sweet it is to
the touch. Yet, even then, that memory, the one where God
had done something to his soul, something worth telling, this
is what he wanted us to hear.

And I think I know why. This book you're holding is my way of doing the same. As you read it, you heard from me what God had done. Loving me, He gave me life. Gave me a heart that was brand new, beating for no other reason than to love Him with all of it. And with this new heart in love with an unchanging God, it compelled me to *tell*.

I didn't want you to come and hear about me. I'm not the one who's done anything *for* my soul. I'd only done things *to* it. But what God has done to my soul is worth telling because He is worth knowing. Worth seeing. Worth hearing. Worth loving, and trusting, and exalting. For my telling is, as I've said before, my praise. To tell you about what God has done for my soul is to invite you into my worship.

> I think we delight to praise what we enjoy because the praise not merely expresses but completes the enjoyment; it is its appointed consummation. It is not out of compliment that lovers keep on telling one another how beautiful they are; the delight is incomplete till it is expressed. It is frustrating to have discovered a new author and not to be able to tell anyone how good he is; to come suddenly, at the turn of the road, upon some mountain valley of unexpected grandeur and then to have to keep silent because the people with you care for it

no more than for a tin can in the ditch; to hear a good joke and find no one to share it with. . . . The Scotch catechism says that man's chief end is "to glorify God and enjoy Him forever." But we shall then know that these are the same thing. Fully to enjoy is to glorify. In commanding us to glorify Him, God is inviting us to enjoy Him.[16]

When the psalmist invited us to come and hear, he was inviting us to enjoy the goodness of God *with* him. This book is no different. Every word, sentence, and paragraph are an explanation of how good God has been to me. Him being good to me is not particular. It's His person. It's Who He is, what He has always been, and Who He will always be. So because He is the same God that did something wonderful to the soul of the psalmist, and the same God that did an equally beautiful thing to my own, He is, even now, more than able to do the same for every soul alive.

---

[16] C. S. Lewis, *Reflections on the Psalms* (1958; repr., San Diego, CA: Harcourt Books, 1986), 95–97.